MARCO ⊕ POLO

Travel with **Insider Tips**

MENORCA

FRANCE

SWITZER LAND

Bilbao

ITALY

ANDORRA

MC

Madrid

Barcelona

Corsica (F)

SPAIN

Menorca

Valencia

Mallorca

Sardinia (I)

Balearic Islands

Mediterranean Sea

ALGERIA

D0736290

SYMBOLS

 Insider Tip

★ Highlight

●●●● Best of...

⌲ Scenic view

◈ Responsible travel: for ecological or fair trade aspects

(*) Telephone numbes that are not toll-free

PRICE CATEGORIES HOTELS

Expensive over 160 euros

Moderate 80–160 euros

Budget under 80 euros

Prices are for a double room in peak season. Breakfast is usually included

PRICE CATEGORIES RESTAURANTS

Expensive over 30 euros

Moderate 15–30 euros

Budget under 15 euros

Prices are for starter, main course and dessert including table wine

On the cover: White beaches & turquoise water p. 69 | Explore the underworld p. 94

CONTENTS

MAPS IN THE GUIDEBOOK
(126 A1) Page numbers and coordinates refer to the road atlas
(0) Site/address located off the map
Coordinates are also given for places that are not marked on the road map
(U A1) Coordinates refer to the street maps of Maó and Ciutadella inside the back cover

(*A–B 2–3*) refers to the removable pull-out map
(*a–b 2–3*) refers to the additional map on the pull-out map

INSIDE FRONT COVER:
The best Highlights

INSIDE BACK COVER:
Street maps of Maó and Ciutadella

The best MARCO POLO Insider Tips

Our top 15 Insider Tips

INSIDER TIP **Tasty medicine**
Menorcan *chamomile flowers* are a well-known traditional panacea and – in case you're not a fan of Chamomile tea – is really tasty as chamomile liqueur → **p. 31**

INSIDER TIP **First class views of the port**
From the end of the short alleyway *Carrer d'Alfons III*, beneath the Pont d'es Castell, you will find the best view of extensive Port de Maó and its many boats (photo right) → **p. 39**

INSIDER TIP **One too many**
The first vintage left the fledgling *Binifadet vineyard* in 2004, but hardly anyone knows that the bodega offers wine tastings and tours (photo above) → **p. 49**

INSIDER TIP **Casino with atmosphere**
To avoid any misunderstandings: the *Casino Sant Climent* is not a gaming casino, but an atmospheric bar and restaurant → **p. 47**

INSIDER TIP **Relax in a historic villa**
Old stone walls, peacocks strutting around the garden and organic, home-grown produce served for breakfast, the *Son Granot* finca is a fine place to relax and feel good → **p. 35**

INSIDER TIP **Hearty convent fare**
Pilgrims and holidaymakers can enjoy good, hearty food in the *Posada del Toro* on Monte Toro – the island's highest mountain → **p. 60**

INSIDER TIP **High C in the cloister**
Delightful sounds fill the otherwise quiet cloister of the old seminary in Ciutadella during the summer music festival, the *Festival de Música d'Estiu* → **p. 110**

INSIDER TIP **On the town walls**
From the *Bastió des Governador* in Ciutadella you can cast your gaze as far as the lighthouse at the mouth of the port → **p. 80**

INSIDER TIP Walking with a sheep
On the "Sunday of the Sheep" at the start of the *St John the Baptist* celebrations in June, a farmer's son carries a lamb on his shoulders through Ciutadella → **p. 110**

INSIDER TIP Sweet seduction
You can get *turrón* – the sweet almond and honey speciality typical of the Balearic Islands – in all its delicious varieties at the specialists *El Turronero* in the centre of Maó → **p. 43**

INSIDER TIP Elegant country hotel serving slow food
Surrounded by vines, olive groves and palm trees, the *Ca Na Xini* country hotel gives you the real taste of Menorca in the middle of nature offering traditional cheeses, quince jelly and wines → **p. 68**

INSIDER TIP Paradise for foodies
The delicatessen *Granel* in Ciutadella serves up a true feast for the eyes and taste buds → **p. 82**

INSIDER TIP Mediterranean delights
The *Brasserie & Bar Dos Pablos* may be run by English owners – but this lovely restaurant in Alaior serves the very best of Mediterranean cuisine → **p. 65**

INSIDER TIP Lodgings with bags of charme
Carefully selected, charming furnishings, only seven intimate rooms and an enthusiastic owner make you feel immediately at home in the *Casa Alberti,* Maó's aristocratic palace dating from 1740 → **p. 45**

INSIDER TIP Hikes for those with steady nerves
The adventurous hiking tours through the unspoilt *Barranc d'Algendar* are ideal for both hiking fans and nature lovers – experienced guides ensure that no one gets lost → **p. 104**

BEST OF...

GREAT PLACES FOR FREE
Discover new places and save money

● *Green view from the tower*
The largest environmental organisation on the island *(GOB Menorca)* has its base in the capital at the *Molí del Rei* (the king's mill) which has splendid views of Maó town and harbour. Admission is free → p. 38

● *Essential needs*
You can sample wine and cheese on the *Hort de Sant Patrici* estate free for the first tasting. If you like the taste, you can buy some more quite cheaply – but there is no obligation to do so → p. 68

● *Green and free*
You can visit the protected wetlands *S'Albufera d'es Grau* – with its rich variety of flora and fauna – on your own or as part of a group tour, and the best thing about it is that the guides are free (photo) → p. 58

● *Free open-air observatory*
Some places on the north coast are so free of light pollution that after sunset you can see thousands of stars with the naked eye. One of the best places not only for hobby astronomers is *Punta Nati* on the north-western tip of the island → p. 88

● *Free wireless internet connection*
Although you are usually charged for using WiFi on Menorca, the local government is now setting up free WiFi zones on all of the Balearic beaches – the project is called "IB-WiFi Playas" → p. 117

● *Parking is free at the beach*
Access and parking at most of the island's unspoilt beaches is once again free of charge. And you can save the 5 euros parking fee for *Calas Macarella* and *Macarelleta* by using the first car park (not far from the beach) and taking a short walk → p. 87

ONLY ON MENORCA
Unique experiences

● *On horseback*
Explore Menorca's quiet side by taking a family trip on horseback through its picturesque countryside and pristine beaches. You can hire horses at *Cavalls Son Àngel* near Playas de Algaiarens → **p. 109**

● *Agritourism*
You can enjoy a particularly stylish and atmospheric stay in one of the old country houses that have been converted into ho-tels, such as the *Binigaus Vell*: old Menorcan tools, rough plastered walls in gleaming white and modern 4-star comforts → **p. 72**

● *Lobster stew*
Not a cheap pleasure, but the original *caldereta* – preferably served in an earthenware *olla* – in a restau-rant such as *Es Port* in Fornells, is as much a part of a Menorca holiday as the missing corners of the island's cheese → **p. 54**

● *Menorca bridle path*
The *Camí de Cavalls* (a network of historic horse trails) was created to move troops quickly. Then the landowners blocked the rights of way. Today the Camí de Cavalls is accessible for everyone: a total of 184 km/ 114 miles of hiking trails through the most beautiful countryside on the island (photo) → **p. 23**

● *In search of everyday Menorcan cuisine*
Erected in the middle of the 19th century and renovated in 2011, the *Mercat* (market) in Ciutadella, tiled in green and white, has a timeless quality. Here you can look over the shoulders of Menorcan women as they go about their shopping → **p. 79**

● *The cradle of civilisation*
Menorca has lots of prehistoric relics, and some of the most impressive are the settlement ruins at *Torre d'en Galmés,* inhabited around 1300 BC by some 600 people → **p. 66**

● *Carribean flair*
Completely typical of Menorca's sunny south side are the ravines which run out into small coves with fine, white sand against the backdrop of the turquoise sea. A good example is *Cala Trebalúger* near Cala Galdana → **p. 70**

ONLY ON

BEST OF...

AND IF IT RAINS?
Activities to brighten your day

● **Jazz in the cellar vaults**
In the cosy *Ars Café* in Maó they serve not only delicious tapas and tasty island wines, but from time to time there are also jazz sessions → **p. 40**

● **Cave paintings**
In Cala Santandria you can visit the *cave dwelling* of the Menorcan sculptor Nicolau Cabrisas. Over the years he imaginatively decorated its interior (photo) → **p. 87**

● **Spain's oldest opera house**
Built in 1829, the treasured *Teatre* in Maó is so small that you can almost touch the artists on the stage. The music performed ranges from classic to jazz and even opera in November → **p. 44**

● **History and anecdotes**
Menorcan history, traditional crafts, paintings and engravings by Menorcan artists: the *Museu de Menorca* in Maó offers lots of diversions → **p. 38**

● **Gift of God, not only for rainy days**
In good weather people only pay it a cursory visit, and yet the impressive *Ciutadella Cathedral* is one of the island's most important Gothic monuments → **p. 78**

● **History in the granary**
In the *Museu Municipal* in Ciutadella – where grain was once stored in the Bastió de Sa Font – you can now quietly browse through Menorcan history → **p. 78**

● **A quieter spot for souvenir shopping**
Menorca's *Centre Artesanal* is located in the quiet resort of Es Mercadal where you will find original, one-off pieces produced by local craftsmen to take home as souvenirs → **p. 108**

RAIN

RELAX AND CHILL OUT
Take it easy and spoil yourself

● *Relaxing for two*
The *Hotel Audax Spa & Wellness* in Cala Galdana is aimed primarily at young people and couples: swimming pools, sauna, jacuzzi and comprehensive beauty and wellness treatments → **p. 69**

● *To "cock pigeon island"*
Take a boat from the quayside at Es Grau to the tiny offshore island of *Illa d'en Colom,* which is home to marine birds and lizards. There are two wonderful beaches on the island where you can enjoy a picnic while gazing over to Menorca → **p. 58**

● *Sundowner at the quayside*
Round off your day in style with a glass of Menorcan wine at one of the *street bars* in Es Castell while watching the boats leave the harbour for the wide open seas → **p. 35**

● *A day at the beach*
The *Cales Coves* ("cave bays") offer an ideal spot for relaxation: Protected from the wind by the surrounding cliffs, the water in the bay is calm and crystal clear. Enjoy a fun day at the beach here (photo) → **p. 48**

● *Spa with special bonus*
The *Barceló Pueblo Menorca* in Punta Prima has some attractive discounts for those who want to use the spa and gym facilities more than once. It is worth asking about them! → **p. 51**

● *Spanish Carribean*
The 20-minute trek on foot to *Cala Mitjana* is well worth the effort: a fine sandy white beach with shallow, turquoise water awaits you. Hidden among pine trees in a rocky bay, it offers a delightful spot for bathing and a picni → **p. 70**

● *Easygoing beachside barr*
At the Sant Adeodat beach in *Es Bruc* on Menorca's south coast you can enjoy reasonably-priced fresh seafood in a relaxed setting, topped off with splendid views out to sea → **p. 72**

DISCOVER MENORCA!

Menorca is the *nice quiet one* compared with her rather loud and cheeky sister islands. It is the furthest Balearic island from the coast of Spain and was connected to the mainland later than Mallorca and Ibiza. As a result, the island has escaped the worst excesses of mass tourism, offering peace and privacy rather than high rises and wild partying. Visitors appreciate Menorca's idyllic bays, stunning beaches, romantic old towns and mysterious remains from antiquity.

Menorca has so much to offer, especially for *lovers of nature*. Around 40 per cent of the island is forested and in the north of the island there are pine and Aleppo forests in great wooded areas. And the variety of animal and plant species is impressive: in the *barrancs*, the dry ravines, there are up to 200 types of plants, of which 25 are endemic to Menorca. There are also some animal species that are at home in the natural habitat of Menorca. The *cavalls*, for example, belong to a breed of horse which is only found on the island, and the island has even been declared a *genetic reservoir* for ten species of animals and four plants species, including the reddish brown dairy cows, red kites, eagles and falcons, turtles and a small species of vulture.

Ambient location: Fortalesa Isabel II on the peninsula of La Mola at the entrance to the harbour of Maó

Menorca is – as Paul Fallot, one of the leading island geographers, once humorously observed – not dissimilar to the shape of a huge broad bean. The island also reminded him of a kidney-shaped table. In fact the island has *two very diferent sides*. Tramuntana in the north is characterised by *calas,* deep fjords which have carved their way into the interior, bizarre rock formations and an irregular coastline with a series of natural harbours. Here the landscape is dominated by dark rocks which, shaped by wind and sea, give many parts of the coastline a *rugged character* and the area has always been more scarcely populated than the centre and the south coast. The north belonged to mythical creatures and gods. There are numerous island legends attached to sites along the windswept north coast while in the north-western parts of the island one encounters large areas of pasture land. Golden cornfields and flowers transform the landscape in spring and autumn into a *spectacular blaze of colour*. The vegetation often extends right down to the coast, clinging ever more tightly to the rocky soil. Only the outermost tips of land, the

Fiords, mythical creatures, cornfields and beaches

2800 BC
Traces of the first settlement, megalithic structures, earliest chamber tombs or *naus (navetas)*

1500 BC
Talaiot culture:
Construction of large cult buildings and walled towns

205 BC
Hannibal's brother, General Magon, arrives on Menorca and establishes Maó

From 123 BC
Roman occupation and decline of the *talaiot* culture

903–1287
Arab occupation; Menorca is annexed to the Caliphate of Córdoba

capes, are completely barren. Here, on stormy days in the autumn or spring, the sea spray showers the dark coastal cliffs with a white deposit of salt.

The Migjorn in the south is completely different, with a more sheltered coastline made up of small bays, wooded valleys and gorges. The southern part of Menorca consists of a 50–60 m/160–200 ft high limestone plateau which gently slopes to the south and is only interrupted by the course of drainage channels. This is where *Menorca's sunny side shows itself*, with a lighter, more Mediterranean architecture and pine trees rising up into the sky, largely sheltered from the strong winds from the Gulf of Lion which, on more than a hundred days in the year, sweep across the north of the island at speeds of more than 100 km/60 mph. Most of the beaches are situated in the south, which is why most tourists are drawn there.

With a total surface area of 270 square miles Menorca is about one and a half times the size of Ibiza, but only a fifth of the size of Mallorca. 70,000 people live here. From Cap Sa Mola to Cap de Bajolí,

Mallorca's little sister, Ibiza's big cousin

the island extends over a length of 47 km/30 miles, with a width of 10–19 km/6–12 miles. About 30 uninhabited islands, some of them tiny, are scattered off the 220 km/140 miles long coastline. Menorca is separated from its big sister Mallorca to the west by a mere 45 km/28 miles at the narrowest point between Cap d'Artrutx and Cap Freu. The Catalan metropolis of Barcelona is 241 km/150 miles away, Africa only 380 km/240 miles, which explains the *mild average temperatures* of more than 25°C/77°F in summer and 14°C/57°F in winter, with more than *2450 hours of sunshine* a year.

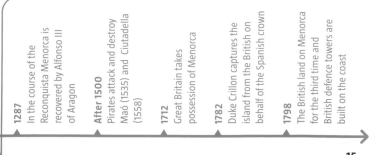

1287
In the course of the Reconquista Menorca is recovered by Alfonso III of Aragon

After 1500
Pirates attack and destroy Maó (1535) and Ciutadella (1558)

1712
Great Britain takes possession of Menorca

1782
Duke Crillon captures the island from the British on behalf of the Spanish crown

1798
The British land on Menorca for the third time and British defence towers are built on the coast

The two sides of the island are also as different as the north and south coast. In the east there is the punctilious, hard-working *Maó*, and in the west the more rebellious and permissive *Ciutadella*. The differences are not only in the architecture, but also in the outlook on life. The rivalry between the two towns has been smouldering for centuries and even today a native of Ciutadella is never happy to go to Maó and will usually only do to for the sake of business or unavoidable bureaucratic procedures. The native of Maó adopts a rather superior air, happy to comment in the capital on news from the western province with a meaningful raise of the eyebrows.

Menorca's historical roots go deep into the past. People are believed to have inhabited the island more than 6500 years ago, the *first settlers* settlers probably having come across the sea on reed boats. Some rock wall drawings in the caves of Menorca depict boats which bear a strong resemblance to similar illustrations on Crete. The oldest remains – imperishable stone buildings assembled without mortar – are up to *4000 years old*. Some of them are still awaiting interpretation, especially the prehistoric caves *(coves)* and settlements *(poblats prehistòrics)* with their stone tables *(taules)* and towers *(talaiots)*, as well as the chamber tombs *(navetas)* which are shrouded in legend and probably the *oldest preserved buildings in Europe*. The island must have experienced its first golden age around the 15th century BC when, within a relatively short period of time, no fewer than 1500 megalithic structures and the first large settlements were established. Later Phoenicians, Greeks, Carthaginians and Romans used the island's strategic location while the Byzantines and finally the Arabs subjugated it.

> **Stone relics bear witness to an ancient past**

It was not until 1287, as the final act of the *Christian reconquest* of Spain as it were, that Menorca was once more wrested from the hands of the "infidels" – which, for the inhabitants of the island at that time, was not necessarily a turn for the better. Famine and epidemics were the consequence and it was only the occupation of Menorca by the British which re-established trade, craft and culture. The island's records for 1784 include 21 goldsmiths and 150 shoemakers and by the end of the 19th century almost 40 per cent of all Menorcans were dependent on shoe production. Today the major exports are *shoes, costume jewellery and cheese*. Fishing and agri-

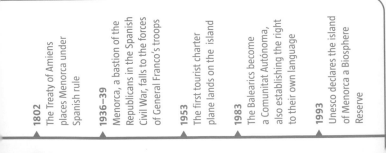

1802
The Treaty of Amiens places Menorca under Spanish rule

1936–39
Menorca, a bastion of the Republicans in the Spanish Civil War, falls to the forces of General Franco's troops

1953
The first tourist charter plane lands on the island

1983
The Balearics become a Comunitat Autónoma, also establishing the right to their own language

1993
Unesco declares the island of Menorca a Biosphere Reserve

Menorca's splendid beaches and bays are the island's hallmark, such as Cala Mitjana

culture is becoming less important while service industries are becoming more so. Today around 60 per cent of all the islanders are directly or indirectly involved in tourism, with some 1.3 million passengers arriving at Menorca's airport every year. And yet there is a determination to place more emphasis on *environmental-conscious individual holidaymakers* rather than on mass tourism. It seems that Menorca is consciously seeking to avoid making the mistakes of its big and little sisters to the south-west. It understands the *Reserva de la Biosfera* designation not just as a clever marketing ploy, and very much wants to prove that a reasonable amount of tourism can be perfectly suited to intact social and cultural structures and a *largely unspoilt natural landscape*. In keeping with the motto: holidays need not make you feel guilty!

> **Environmentally-conscious individual holidays**

2001
In August a record 350,000 foreigners and 150,000 Spaniards visit the island

2005
Menorca is the first of the Balearic islands to commit itself to "Local Agenda 21", the pro-gramme for sustainable development

2015
Environmental activists and the Balearic government successfully campaign against boring for crude oil in the west of the Mediterranean

WHAT'S HOT

1 Natural fashion

Eco-fashion Clothes that you can wear with a clear conscience. That's the fashionable credo of the Menorcans. T-shirts, shorts or caps from ◉ *Ecologic Line Trendwear (at Blau Mari, C/ Major des Born, 5 | Ciutadella (photo)* are made from organic cotton, and also make a nice souvenir. The items are decorated with typical Menorcan motifs.

The creative team at ◉ *Avarques (C/ Ses Moreres 47 | Maó and C/ Calles Fonts 30 | Es Castell | www.avarcashop.com)* also have the environment and design in mind with their selection of trendy shoes.

2 Hill and dale

Bike More and more holidaymakers want to explore the island by bike, and the ever increasing demand is being met by companies such as *Anthony's Bikes (C/ Xaloc | Alaior | www.anthonysbikes.com)* that rent out mountain bikes. Route tips can be found at *www.menorca.es.* If you have the stamina, you can take part in the *Volta a Menorca* in October, a round-the-island bike race *(www.menorcabtt.com).*

3 A fine drop of wine

Wine From time immemorial grapes have been processed here into wine. However, it is only in recent years that the island has become an internationally renowned wine area – thanks to its new winemakers. At *Sa Cudia (Ctra. Es Grau, km 8 | Maó) (photo)* the Malvasia grape is used to produce a fruity, floral white wine. The quality wines at *Ferrer de Muntpalau (Camí de Tramuntana, km 1 | Es Mercadal | www.lasenciadelvino.com)* are also available internationally. *ViMenorca (www.vimenorca.com)* has set itself the goal of co-ordinating all the winegrowers' activities. *www.bodegasmenorquinas.com.*

On water

By kayak Some isolated beaches can only be accessed from the sea. If you do not seek them out, you will be missing out on a great little adventure. Rent a kayak at *Katayak Kayak (bookings: tel. 6 26 48 64 26 | www.katayak.net)* – they'll also give you tips on where to go – and set off to sea. *DMW Sports & Kayak (bookings: tel. 6 18 72 01 72 | www.sports kayak.es) (photo)* provide extended guided excursions and also express kayaking courses. Perfect for beginners! There is also *Dia Complert (Av. Passeig Maritim 41 | tel. 6 09 67 09 96 | www.diacomplert.com)* in Fornells that offer both activities on land, as well as guides who take kayakers through caves and to the most beautiful coastal sections – on request you can also take a break to snorkel or sunbathe on a secluded beach.

Private accomodation

Amongst locals in low-key, charming residences located in the centre of the old town. Residents of Menorca's old and new capital cities, Ciutadella and Maó respectively, are catching on to the trend of transforming historic homes into stylish and comfortable guest rooms and apartments, allowing visitors to feel more like guests rather than anonymous tourists. The "Three Saints" in Ciutadella offers particularly delightful accommodation *(Tres Sants | 8 rooms | C/ Sant Sebastiá 2/ San Cristófol | tel. 9 71 48 22 08 | Moderate)* as does the "Small Maó" in Maó *(Petit Maó | 6 rooms | C/ Infanta 17 | tel. 6 61 02 02 54 | www. hotelpetitmao.com | Moderate)*.

IN A NUTSHELL

ARABS

As almost all of Spain, Menorca was also once occupied by the Arabs. From AD 903 the island was part of the Caliphate of Córdoba and remained under Islamic rule for nearly 400 years. It wasn't until January 1287 that King Alfonso III of Aragon succeeded in re-conquering under Christian rule. The Arab population was enslaved, their belongings plundered and their buildings razed. This is why today there are so few architectural indications on Menorca of the centuries of Muslim rule. The Arab inheritance, however, remained alive in the form of place names. The prefix *bini*, for example, means a possession "of the son of...", and the words *rafál* or *cúdia* refer to a house, a hut, a place on a hill.

ARCHITECTURE

In the towns you will find impressive examples of Catalan gothic (Ciutadella Cathedral) and baroque (Del Socors church in Ciutadella, Ferreries church and others). Many of the town houses in Maó and also Ciutadella reveal attractive elements of art nouveau *(modernisme)*. The rural homesteads are quite striking, distinctive and bold, usually dominating the surrounding land from a hilltop. They are almost always whitewashed and have lots of smaller adjoining buildings. One remarkable feature is the clay gutters and downpipes, sometimes running diagonally across the whole facade, which collect water into subterranean cisterns. As wind and rain (especially in the north of the island) destroy the facades which are usually made of *marés*

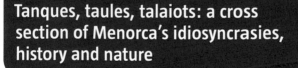

Tanques, taules, talaiots: a cross section of Menorca's idiosyncrasies, history and nature

(sandstone), the island inhabitants protect their homes with a thick coating of limestone, which is applied once a year. Nowadays modern emulsion paint is used, sometimes applied even to the roof.

BARRANCS

Barrancs or *barrancos* in Spanish are narrow ravines carved by rain has into the soft limestone over thousands of years. Protected from the north wind by 20–40 m/65–130 ft high cliff walls, some of these places on Menorca became early centres of settlement. This is where the island's most fertile fields and some of the most species-rich biotopes (with up to 200 types of plant) are to be found. There are 36 *barrancs* on the geologically younger southern side of Menorca. Many of the beautiful bays on the south coast are also offshoots of such ravines. The ones absolutely worth seeing are the Barranc d'Algendar between Ferreries and Cala Galdana, the Barranc de Trebalúger to the east and the *barrancs* at Son Bou, Es Bec and Son Boter.

Cala Pregonda is also part of the Biosphere Reserve

BIOSPHERE RESERVE

The Unesco "Man and the Biosphere" committee agreed in 1993 to Menorca's request to being a *Reserva de la Biosfera*. The request was preceded by a meticulous study of the environment and the cultural, social, ecological, agricultural and tourist issues, because the precondition for the Unesco rating is not only an unspoilt natural world, but also evidence that man is able to live in the area without compromising or destroying it. *Reserva de la Biosfera* is a dynamic process by which the island, year after year, has to prove that economics and ecology, tourism and the environment can co-exist compatibly.

BRITISH

The British have conquered and occupied Menorca three times in the course of history, the first time occurring during the Spanish War of Succession. In 1706 Joan Saura on Menorca supported the claims of the Austrian Archduke Charles and managed to win over the majority of the island's communities to his cause. The island governor Diego Dávila barricaded himself in the San Felipe fortress and suppressed the rebellion with French support in 1707.

But when Anglo-Dutch troops landed in Cala d'Alcalfar in the autumn of 1708, the governor surrendered virtually without a fight, paving the way for 48 years of British rule. After the French conquest in 1756, Great Britain regained the island in the Treaty of Paris of 1763. In the following 19 years under British sovereignty the coast garrison of Georgetown (today: Es Castell) was founded. In 1782 Franco-Spanish troops conquered the island once more. However, 16 years later the Spaniards were ousted by a renewed British invasion that landed on the north coast in 1798. This last period of British rule lasted only four years until the Treaty of Amiens of 1802 finally placed the island under Spanish rule. Almost a century of British rule left its mark on Menorca.

CAMÍ DE CAVALLS

The "horse path", which goes right round the entire island, dates back to an ancient right of way. After the re-conquest of the islands, King James II of Mallorca instructed the Menorcans to be ready to defend any part of the island at any time, on horseback and armed with a lance. In order to dispatch troops quickly to the coast, an extensive network of well-made paths was necessary, their maintenance being the duty of the individual property owners.

With the extension of modern roads in the interior, the horse path fell into disuse by the beginning of the 20th century and many of the 120 property owners closed their section of the trail. Countless court judgements and one of the largest demonstrations in the island's history were necessary to achieve the reinstatement of the ancient rights of way. In 2010 the ● *Camí de Cavalls* was once again open to the public for walking, horse riding or cycling. This means that a total of 184 km/115 miles of nature trails through some of the most beautiful landscapes on the island are now available. For routes and maps see: *www.camidecavalls360.com*

FAUNA

Some species occur only – or are exceptionally abundant – on Menorca. These include the *moixeta*, a small white vulture which is mainly to be found on the north coast and is the only one of its kind which doesn't undertake a winter migration southwards; the red kite, which nests mainly on the steep coastal slopes and the high canopy of large forests; and the short-legged Balearic shrew which is extremely shy and lives in the shadows and in wall crevasses.

FRENCH

A nephew of Cardinal Richelieu, Marshal Armand de Vignerot du Plessis, Duke of Richelieu, granted Menorca a seven-year French intermezzo from 1756 which, in spite of its short duration, made history. For example, the township of Sant Lluís dates back to a French founder; mayonnaise, the best-selling sauce in the world, is said to have been inspired by the marshal himself; and hiking fans have to thank the French for extending and improving the *Camí de Cavalls*, the long-

WORLD FAMOUS DIP

Whole volumes have already been written on the origins of one of the most popular sauces in the world. Quite a few trails lead to Menorcan cuisine. In fact, the French Marshal Richelieu may well have helped mayonnaise enjoy its world-wide popularity. Rumour has it that a *mahonesa*, a woman from Maó, stole the marshal's heart and in return revealed to him some of the secrets of Menorcan cuisine. One of the local culinary customs the lady showed him was a simple, rustic recipe: olive oil, blended with egg, a pinch of salt and crushed garlic. It is quite possible that the noble French mayonnaise is related to the Balearic *all i oli* (garlic with oil), the *mahonesa's* sauce, without the garlic.

est and, in parts, most beautiful hiking trail on the island.

MENORQUÍ

Menorquí, the Menorcan language, is one of the oldest dialects of *català*, Catalan. It is still in use today, one of the nine Romance languages introduced to the Balearics in 1287 by King Alfonso III of Aragon. In fact, all the occupying powers, Romans and Arabs, French and British, have left their linguistic trace. In particular, lots of English words are in everyday use. For example, they talk about shutting the *vindou*, eating *bifi* for lunch, served on the *tibord (tea board)*, or after a quick drink they say they *ha fet un trinqui*. *Català* has been recognised since 1983 as an official language on the Balearics with equal status to Castilian Spanish and now enjoys great popularity amongst the younger generation after the years of suppression of all regional languages under the Franco dictatorship. Place names on road signs are now almost only still in the Catalan variant. In addition to *menorquí*, you will also hear *castellano (Castilian Spanish)* and often also English.

NATURE CONSERVATION

In 1991 a comprehensive Nature Conservation Act became law on the Balearics, achieving its final form in 1992. Since then 42.67 per cent of Menorca's surface is under protection (the European average is approx. 7 per cent). The most extensive protected areas include the coastline (exceptions: the area around Ciutadella and the area south of Maó), a large part of Tramuntana, the northern half of the island, but also large areas around Alaior, Cales Coves and Es Migjorn Gran. The Grup Balear de Ornitologia i Defensa de la Naturalesa (GOB) *(www.gobmenorca. com)* has been involved in animal and environmental protection on the Balearics since 1971.

In 2001 all 20 municipalities became affiliated to Local Agenda 21 and since 2009 the communities have been working to implement the action plans. Local Agenda 21 is based on a UN agreement for sustainable development at community level, meaning that communities are required to manage their social, ecological and economic matters in such a way the environment is maintained for future generations.

PREHISTORIC STRUCTURES

"Talaiot" (2500–123 B.C.) is the name used to describe the society that existed on Menorca during the Iron Age which erected impressive megaliths. Although these monuments can be found on the other Balearic islands, Menorca has the most with a total of 1600 sites, 274 of which are well-maintained remains. They are spread across the island with the most found in the island's fertile south. The word *talaiot* originates from the Arabic word *atalaya* (lookout tower) and indeed most of the monuments are situated on mounts. There are three types of constructions: *talaiots* ("lookout towers"), *taules* ("tables") and *navetas* ("ships") shaped like a ship's hull facing keel-side up. It is presumed that these were used as graves. *Talaiots* are round or rectangular-shaped structures made of large stones without the use of mortar. The *taules* can be up to 3 m in height and consist of vertical pillars with a horizontal stone lying on them. Although their exact meaning is unknown, one theory is they were the place where Celtic Druids performed human sacrifices. It is more likely, however, that the *taules* themselves represented a deity, for example a bull. The central stone T is almost always surrounded by a circle of monoliths. The whole complex, where a fire constantly burned and animal sacrifices were made, was almost certainly used for ritual purposes.

RICHARD KANE

This is a name you come across frequently in Menorca. Richard Kane was appointed governor in 1722; 14 years after the British first occupied the island. Since it was primarily the inhabitants of Ciutadella who were against the conquerors, Kane summarily made Maó, the town in the east, the island capital. Rights and land tenure were to a large extent respected, and the changes which the new governor instigated were more of a practical nature. And so, for example, he had a new road built, the *Camí d'en Kane*, between Maó and Ciutadella (20 km/12.5 miles, today a popular hiking path), curtailed the power of the Inquisition and introduced new crops (such as apples) and new breeds of cattle. He is also said to have been responsible for the development of Menorca's dairy industry. Whilst the clergy and the nobility retreated in a sulk to Ciutadella, the respect of the rural population for the governor grew – something which his successors Anstruther, Wynyard and Murray failed to emulate.

TANQUES

This is the name given to those fields on Menorca which are surrounded by dry stone walls and usually closed by a gate. The total length of all the dry stone walls on the island amounts to about 15,000 km/9000 miles.

Talaiots at Binisafúller on the island's south coast are prehistoric places of worship

FOOD & DRINK

Bon profit! **Even if the prices of some** *caldereta* **suggest the opposite – this enthusiastic greeting is not uttered for the landlord's benefit, rubbing his hands eagerly as he presents you with the bill, but is simply expressing the wish that you will enjoy your meal.**

On Menorca there are some ***540 restaurants*** (with seating for more than 30,000) as well as a good 660 bars and cafés. The Balearic authorities provide a rather superficial quality classification – referring mainly to cleanliness, furnishing and seating capacity – for restaurants (forks as a symbol), bars (goblets) and cafeterias (cups). One symbol indicates a basic standard and three the very best quality. Just under a third of the premises on Menorca are ***pure*** ***holiday businesses***, closing down when the season comes to an end, and they generally provide more or less good "international" cuisine, i.e. steak, chicken, hamburgers and occasionally fish, usually with a generous portion of chips and some salad. Once you've tried it, you know pretty well how it is going to taste everywhere else, and you may then be more curious to find out what else is simmering in the island's *greixoneres* and *olles* (clay pots and bowls). It is worth being a bit adventurous, you will not be disappointed. ***Menorca's cuisine is simple, rich, hearty*** and very tasty. Cultures which were historically incompatible come together in the saucepan, simple Arab and Catalan recipes, for example, are given a British touch or enhanced by

The table spread is produce from the sea and fields: simple, honest, rooted in nature – Menorca's authentic cuisine is back in favour

a subtle soupçon of French flair. **Everything that is served comes from the sea and the fields**, including typical vegetables such as tomatoes, artichokes, peas, beans, onions, potatoes, carrots and cabbage. And there is game, lamb, veal, pork and lots of fresh fish and other seafood – all preferably prepared with garlic, olive oil and the island's aromatic herbs such as rosemary and thyme.

Caldereta is now a very upmarket meal. It is **red lobster cooked in a delicate ve-**getable broth (the basic recipe is: onion, two cloves of garlic, tomato, leek, seasoned with two tablespoons of brandy and a sprig of parsley). A portion costs about 80 euros, but for this rather steep price you are invited to select your own live lobster, which is then transformed into culinary delicacy in the saucepan.

As soon as you arrive at the airport you will encounter piles of *ensaïmadas*, a delicious, light, spiral-shaped **pastry**. It comes in various sizes and with different fillings, such as *cabello de ángel* (pump-

LOCAL SPECIALITIES

Albergínies al forn – baked aubergines, the aubergine halves are filled with a bread, egg, spices and aubergine flesh mixture and baked in the oven

Arròs brut – "dirty rice": rice dish with meat, black pudding, peas, beans, garlic and herbs

Calamar farcit – stuffed squid: gently fried squid that is stuffed with a mixture of coarse bread crumbs, parsley, garlic, egg and pine nuts and then braised in the oven (photo right)

Carabassons al forn – baked courgettes: same preparation as for *albergínies al forn*

Caragols – snails (done the Menorcan way) that are fed for three days on flour, then cooked in a herb stock (made up of bay leaves, garlic, parsley, onions and tomato) and served with aioli

Coca de verdura – yeast dough pizza topped with vegetables

Conill amb cebes – rabbit with onions is usually cooked in a *greixonera*, a typical clay pot. Other varieties alsocombine rabbit with lobster and other seafood

Greixonera de brossat – curd cheese baked in a flat clay pot with lemon zest and cinnamon, a light creamy dessert

Llom amb col – a pork and cabbage stew cooked with white wine, bacon, tomatoes, onions, garlic and thyme in a clay pot

Oli i aigua – a tomato and vegetable soup, served in clay bowls and with thin slices of bread

Olla de mongetes – substantial bean soup with onions, tomatoes, garlic and white beans

Peix en es forn – halibut, redfish or a similar fish is baked in the oven with potatoes, raisins, pine nuts, spinach and tomatoes

Perdiu amb col – guinea fowl breasts are gently fried and then cooked in a clay pot. Cabbage leaves dusted with flour are fried in oil until golden and then served in the clay pot with the guinea fowl

Pilotes – tiny meatballs in a tomato or almond sauce, available in most bars as tapas (photo left)

Sofrit – vegetable dish made of onions, peppers, tomatoes and garlic, as a side dish or as a topping for flat bread *(coques)*

kin jam), *crema* (crème patissière) and *nata* (whipped cream), and is to be found in almost all the bakeries on the island. The most important aspect in making it is that pork lard is used (which gives it its name, as *saïm* means lard). However, *crespells*, though equally sweet and sprinkled with icing sugar, are dry and crumble easily. Just like the *rubiolls*, they are made from a firm biscuit dough which is rolled out and can be filled with pumpkin jam or a sweet crème patissière. And finally there are also the *bunyols,* mainly available in the autumn, which are whorls (similar to small, hand-made doughnuts) made from a semi-liquid dough of flour or potato flour fried in hot oil. *Empanadas,* turnovers filled with vegetables, pork or a meat-vegetable mix, are **hearty and tasty**. During Easter they are also filled with lamb and on Menorca they are then called *formatjades.*

The best of the island's **cold meat products** is the *sobrasada*, a cured pork sausage which acquires its characteristic red colour from red bell peppers. It is often sliced and fried and even combined with honey or *ensaïmadas*. *Butifarrones* (black pudding) and *carn i xulla* (comparable to a coarse pepper salami) are also available everywhere, as is *Queso Maó-Menorca*, the famous **Menorcan cheese**. Just as there is no doubt that the British brought **gin** to Menorca, it is just as certain that that the people of Menorca have acquired a taste for the spirit. A distillery in Port de Maó produces it in the traditional way and there is another distillery which, since 2011, has been offering a Mediterranean variety under the brand name "Gin Mare". A popular and refreshing **island cocktail** is *pellofa,* gin with a generous splash of soda water and a slice of lemon. Copious amounts of *pomada*, a mix of

gin and lemonade, are consumed, especially on feast days.

Herbes (Spanish *hierbas)* comes originally from the Balearic island of Ibiza, further to the west, but Menorca also has some outstanding examples of this sweet, yellow herbal liqueur. The two regional specialities are the typical **Menorcan chamomile liqueur** as well as *palo,* a liqueur made from the fruits of the carob tree.

Good quality: Menorca gin

SHOPPING

Written off as a lost cause, Balearic arts and crafts have in recent years recovered significantly. A good example is Menorca. New, creative spirits are revisiting classic forms, traditional styles and old methods of production. The result is quite impressive: elegant leather shoes or, rather alternative, handmade *avarques* (sandals), leather bags, coats, jackets and trousers for every taste and purse. You can also buy ceramics and ever more frequently artistic woodwork and traditional musical instruments too. The folding chairs covered with linen are also popular, and you can have them made in your favourite colour at *Sillas Menorca (Polígon Industrial de Ferreries | C/ Teulers 16 | www.sillas menorca.com)*. In all the major resorts you will find *bisutería*, i.e. costume jewellery and paste gems. Fashionable accessories have been produced on the island since the 17th century. *Opening times: Mon–Fri 9.30am–1.30pm, 5pm–8pm, Sat mornings only*

ARTS AND CRAFTS

In July and August special arts and crafts markets are held every Wednesday evening (7–11pm) in Alaior and Thursday evening (7–10pm) in Es Mercadal.

CERAMICS

The individual pieces, or in fact the whole dinner service, are almost always hand painted. The predominant patterns are colourful rustic motifs, occasionally also simple British decoration. The pottery is made according to strict, traditional rules and there are only a few young potters who are nowadays prepared to make creative concessions.

CHAMOMILE

Essential oils, resins and glycosides give the dried flower heads of chamomile a medicinal effect. Because of its calming and antibacterial effect, the versatile medicinal plant has been a favourite throughout Europe since ancient times. Menorcan chamomile (Catalan *camamilla*) used to be harvested on the island, especially around Ciutadella, and it was well-known throughout Spain, but today it is gathered by very few people on the island. You can still buy genuine Menorcan chamomile at *Tot Bio (C/ Bonaire 18 | Maó)*.

The many family businesses and cottage enterprises have developed a remarkable penchant for the classic and elegant

CHEESE

It has hardly any aroma, has a semi-firm rind and, because of its square shape, it is easy to store and transport: *Queso Maó-Menorca* (as it is been officially called since 1995). It is marketed under the brand names *Coinga, Sant Patrici* and *La Payesa* amongst others. Menorcan cheese is an ideal holiday gift which you can buy in most grocery stores or from a producer in Alaior. But beware: only about 30 per cent of the cheese is really homemade. The real article can be distinguished from its industrially produced cousins by the cotton cloth pattern (particularly visible at the corners) as well as by its spicier taste.

GIN, PALO, HERBES

Popular souvenirs are local gin – which the British brought to the island – and the dark brown, high-proof speciality *palo*, a liqueur made from melted sugar or carob tree fruit. *Hierbas* or *herbes,* the liqueur containing up to 40 different island herbs, actually comes from Ibiza, but you will find it in every bar on Menorca – which also applies to **INSIDER TIP** chamomile liqueur.

LEATHER

You can find leather goods made on the island in *Maó* at *Pons Quintana (C/ S'Arravaleta 21;* shoes), in *Alaior* at *Gomila (C/ Miguel de Cervantes 46;* shoes) in *Ciutadella* in the leather factory *Patricia (C/ Santandria)* and in their shop in the old town *(C/Josep Cavalier i Piris 5 | www.patricia.es)*. *Mascaro* produces fashionable, high quality leather accessories; they have shops at the airport, in *Ferreries (Polígono Industrial)* and in *Maó (C/ Ses Moreres 29 | www.jaimemascaro.es)*.

MAÓ/
EASTERN TIP

For centuries there has been a smouldering rivalry between the west of Menorca and the east, between the towns of Ciutadella and Maó. Ciutadella had for a long time been the main port and therefore the dominant town but this changed when the British occupied the island and made Maó its capital.

Resistance to the British occupation grew with each new governor, especially amongst the wealthy families who had always lived almost exclusively in Ciutadella. The clergy too, already annoyed at the sudden presence of the competing Anglican faith, resented Governor Richard Kane's interference in the affairs of the strong arm of the church, the Inquisition.

Mao was different – welcoming the British almost as liberators, opening up new trading opportunities. So Richard Kane wasted no time and make Maó the island capital. Today it is the largest urban area on the island, in marked contrast to the remote and rugged north coast, the peaceful Es Grau wetlands, and the narrow trail of sleepy villages winding their way along the south coast.

ES CASTELL

(131 E–F4) (*ΔΔ J–K6*) As you make your way along the mile-long "fjord" which ends in Maó, you will already see the impact British colonial thinking has had

Merry Minorca: Maó has the British to thank for its status as the island's administrative and commercial centre

on the architecture of Es Castell: a rectangular town plan and a central main square surrounded by garrison buildings.

The former crown settlement of Georgetown, later renamed Villacarlos, and now called Es Castell (population 7900) has blossomed into a self-confident community. The port, *Cales Fonts*, is full of life with bars, shops and restaurants, and this is now where some of it happens in the evening rather than in Maó itself.

FOOD & DRINK

CAPRICHOSA
Trendy pizzeria with a sea view, very busy in summer. *C/ Cales Fonts 44 | tel. 9 71 36 61 58 | Moderate*

DINKUM BAR-RESTAURANTE
Ideal for fans of fresh fish. Located in the rocks on the waterfront, overlooking the port and in the evenings there is a romantic candlelit atmosphere. *C/ Cales Fonts 20 | tel. 9 71 36 70 17 | Moderate–Expensive*

EL CHIVITO

This is the ideal place for a light snack: very good value for money, tasty meals and friendly staff. They serve delicious *bocadillos*. Popular with young clientele. *C/ Cales Fonts 25 | tel. 9 71 35 29 44 | Budget*

very reasonable lunch menu. *C/ de Sa Font 1 | tel. 9 71 35 47 88 | Moderate*

SHOPPING

There is a small artisan market on the port steps at *Cales Fonts* from June to

Bars, shops and restaurants line the port at Es Castell

ESPAÑA

This traditional restaurant attracts a crowd with its affordable lunchtime specials while an à la carte menu is served in the evenings: large portions of fresh seafood, homemade desserts and added to that a friendly, efficient service. *C/ Victori 48 | tel. 9 71 36 32 99 | Budget–Moderate*

IRENE

You really get something for your money in this pretty restaurant: international cuisine with fresh, first class ingredients. The ☼ terrace has a stunning, panoramic view of the bay. There is a good and

September *(daily 8pm–2am)*. The *Mercat Artesanal (Mon 7pm–midnight | C/ Miranda des Cales Fonts)* offers exclusive arts & crafts.

SPORTS & ACTIVITIES

You can book a taxi boat to take a private tour around the harbour or to ferry you across to Maó, the La Mola fortress or the island of Illa del Rei: *Water Taxi (May–Oct | tel. 6 16 42 88 91 | minimum of 2 persons, tickets are sold on board)*. Learn how to sail at the *Club Náutico Es Castell (Miranda de Cales Fonts | tel. 9 71 36 58 84)*.

ENTERTAINMENT

Sedate rather than lively: ● Along the pedestrian promenades Moll des Pons and Cales Fonts, small bars built into the rocks with terraces by the sea and a view of the harbour mouth create a pleasant atmosphere for a quiet, sociable evening. The *Chèspir (C/ Cales Fonts 47)* sometimes offers live jazz; *Margarita Café (Moll d'en Pons 6)* is also relaxing. The cave bar *Es Cau (daily from 10pm | C/ Cala Corb 5)* is cult among the Meorcans; for decades they have been playing island folk here.

WHERE TO STAY

EL ALMIRANTE

Admiral Collingwood once resided in this mansion dating from the 18th century; today it is a boutique hotel. Close to the sea, swimming pool and tennis court. *39 rooms | Ctra. Maó-Es Castell | tel. 9 71 36 27 00 | www.hoteldelalmirante. com | Moderate*

INSIDER TIP ► SON GRANOT ☺

This feudal villa built in 1712 for the former chief engineer of the British Empire stands just 500 m/1640 ft away from the harbour. Set in extensive garden grounds with a splendid pool, you can enjoy the surroundings while eating breakfast on the terrace - most of the fresh produce is grown on the finca including organic vegetables, fruit and eggs. You can watch peacocks strutting around the grounds and may even spot a stray hen on the hotel's terrace. The rooms have romantic four-poster queen size beds with balconies which offer amazing views. The villa has a fireplace room with extensive library and riding stables. You can also hire bikes to explore the island. Señora Carolina belongs to the villa and is always on hand with ideas of what to do

in the area. *11 rooms | Ctra. de Sant Felip | tel. 9 71 35 55 55 | www.songranot.com | Moderate–Expensive*

INFORMATION

Ateneu Municipal de Es Castell | C/ Miranda de Cala Corb 10 | tel. 9 71 35 23 66 | turisme@aj-escastell.org

WHERE TO GO

CASTELL DE SANT FELIP
(131 E–F4) (*ʘ K6*)

The road to the cemetery *(Camí del Cementeri)* also leads to the ruins of the fortress which once guarded the entrance to Port de Maó. Spain's King Philip II saw only one means of defence against the constant threat from pirates: the construction of a fortification. Building started in 1554 and was only completed some 54 years later. The British later extended it

★ **Santa Maria**
You can admire the marvellous organ in this church in Maó → p. 39

★ **Tour of Port de Maó**
Cruise by glass-bottom boat through the Mediterranean's largest natural harbour → p. 43

★ **Cales Coves**
The twin bay with its 100 caves has an eventful past → p. 48

★ **Binibèquer Vell**
Fascinating warren of narrow alleys with lots of nooks and crannies: resort design of the future → p. 50

MARCO POLO HIGHLIGHTS

into one of the most secure fortifications in the Mediterranean. It was considered so secure that, on his accession, Charles III ordered its destruction. Today you can see ruins, where nature is slowly but surely taking over again, underground tunnels and corridors *(June–Sept Thu and Sun 10am, otherwise only with pre-booking | adnission 5 euros | tel. 9 71 36 21 00 | www.museomilitarmenorca.com/san-felipe)*.

Another fortress protects the southern shore of the nearby *Cala Sant Esteve*. The British built *Fort Marlborough* here in the 18th century and today, as a museum, it provides a trip back into the past *(see p. 107)*.

ILLA DEL LLATZERET (131 E–F4) *(ɱ K6)*

A huge hospital covers the southern tip of the island which lies in the entrance to the port. From 1817–1917 this was the port quarantine centre. Heavily guarded and protected by massive walls, the hospital must have been witness to some tragic events. In addition to the hospital, which is today used as a spa hotel for officials and as a congress venue, there is a small *museum*. The hospital island can only be visited on certain (variable) weekdays. *lazaretodemahon.es*

MAÓ

MAP INSIDE BACK COVER
(131 E4) *(ɱ J6)* **With a population of only 29,000, Menorca's capital may be small but it is in fact home to approximately half the island's inhabitants. Sitting pretty on one of the world's best natural harbours, Maó is built atop the cliffs with the fjord-like bay below and its pretty villas and Colonial style houses give the city its particular charm.**

Maó has much to offer in the way of culture with some of Menorca's best mu-seums, Spain's oldest opera house and several churches. The city also has a long line of bars, restaurants and clubs to choose from along its regenerated quayside. Visitors to the island should not miss out on a boat trip around the city's harbour. It's worth spending a few days in Maó to get to know the capital's inhabitants. The next beaches are just a few miles away and all of the island's resorts are easily accessible by bus or car. Maó is divided into three distinct parts: the historic centre is in the upper part of the city from where you can head down to the "down at the sea" district (Baix-amar) with its line of restaurants and amusements along the quayside. "On the other side" (S'Altra Banda), i.e. on the fjord's north banks, you'll find more attractions. Most visitors first head to the Plaça de s'Esplanada with its bus station, car park and tourist information. The Car-rer de ses Moreres on the east-side of the square takes you to the Plaça d'Espanya with a set of steps leading down to the harbour. Alternatively you can take the INSIDER TIP free lift next to the hotel *Port Mahon.*

SIGHTSEEING

ATENEU CIENTÌFIC (U A2) *(ɱ a2)*

The culture centre with the warm wooden and geometrically tiled floors is used by the Menorcans for *tertulias* – relaxed social gatherings. Holidaymakers are more interested in the small exhibitions of ceramics, antique maps and fossils. *Mon–Fri 10am–2pm, 4pm–9pm, in summer only mornings | Sa Rovellada de Dalt 25 | near Pl. de S'Esplanada | www.ateneumao.org*

BAIXAMAR (PORT) (U A–E1) *(ɱ a–e1)*

"Julyo, agosto y Maó/los mejores puertos del Mediterraneo son" (July, August and Maó are the safest ports in the Mediterranean). At least this was the rhyme made up by someone who should know: Admiral Andrea Doria. He spoke only in glowing terms of his favourite port: adequate draught, excellent protection from wind and weather for a whole fleet, and good medical provision were amongst the ben-

the island; and then in the evening there are countless nightclubs, bars and pubs, many of them in the former warehouses and boat sheds, where you can spend time late into the night.

Baixamar is, however, not only the spruced up area around the two harbour break-

The quayside of Maó lights up when the sun begins to set

efits of the port channel three miles long and more than 1000 m/3300 ft wide. When necessary the port basin could be sealed off by means of a fortress *(Sant Felip)* – from the military point of view, the perfect port, unique for its size in the Mediterranean.

It is only in more recent times that the landlubbers of Maó have found more civilian uses for the port. It is now for pleasure that you go "down to the sea" to *Baixamar*. The port promenade offers not only an ever increasing range of food and drink, but also a variety of water sport activities, and a broad range of entertainment options. During the day there are souvenir shops, boat trips and the *Xoriguer* gin distillery, famous throughout

waters – *Moll de Ponent* lying to the west which extends east to the *Moll de Llevant* and finally joins *Cala Figuera* – but also the stretch of coast to the north and opposite. This is home to large industrial companies, warehouses and business premises as well as freight ship terminals. This is also where Menorca's only power station is located, which provides part of the island with energy – the rest coming via undersea cable from Mallorca.

CENTRE D'ART I D'HISTORIA HERNÁNDEZ SANZ (U C2) *(🗺 c2)*

Adorned with decorative murals, this restored merchants' house (1805) is a fine example of how Menorca's upper class once lived on the island. Besides its architecture, this museum houses an interesting collection, tracking the development of the harbour under British rule as well as exhibiting expressive paintings and etchings from Menorcan artists. *Daily except Tue 10am–1.30pm, Mon, Wed–Sat also 6–8pm | admission free | C/ Anuncivay 2*

and extended in 2005. Since then it has been used as an ecological information centre, as a shop for Menorcan souvenirs (usually environmentally friendly), and above all as one of the best viewing platforms overlooking the old town and the port. *Mon–Fri 9.30am–2pm and Mon–Thu 5.30pm–8pm | admission free | Camí*

Civilised idleness in Maó's old town

LIBRARIES

There are two good places if you're interested in the printed word: the *Biblioteca Publica*, founded in 1861 (U B1) (*b1*) (*Pl. de la Conquesta 8 | Mon–Fri 9.30am–1.30pm, 5pm–8.30pm, Sat 9.30am–1.30pm, in summer only Mon–Fri mornings*) with internet stations and the smaller *Biblioteca Fernando Rubió i Tudurí* (U C2) (*c2*) (*Pl. del Carme | Mon–Fri 9am–1pm, 5pm–8pm, Sat 10am–1pm, June–Sept closed Sat | www.fundaciorubio.org*).

MOLÍ DEL REI ● 🐾 ☼
(U C2) (*c2*)

The "King's mill" is a mill tower dating from the 18th century, that was restored

des Castell 53 | www.gobmenorca.com/ moli

MUSEU DE MENORCA ●
(U A1) (*a1*)

In the *Sant Francesc* convent there are exhibits of archaeological finds, historic paintings and maps as well as ethnological items and contemporary art – Menorca's richest collection of traditions, customs, history and prehistory. You can also visit the picturesque cloister of the former Franciscan convent, whose origins date back to the 15th century. *April–Oct Tue–Sat 10am–2pm, 6pm–9pm, Sun 10am–2pm, Nov–March Tue–Fri 9.30am–2pm, Sat/ Sun 10am–2pm | Pl. Pla des Monestir*

PLAÇA BASTIÓ (U B1–2) (∅ b1–2)

You get to Plaça Bastió via the gentle climb up *Carrer Sant Roc*. The gate was part of the town wall from the 14th century and the starting point of the long journey to Ciutadella, the western tip of the island. Today the towers are home to various associations, and the square is dominated by bars and cafés.

PLAÇA DEL CARME (U B–C2) (∅ b–c2)

The square is named after the former *Claustre del Carme* convent whose colonnades (erected from 1726) house souvenir and delicatessen shops as well as some vegetable and fruit stands. Most produce is now sold in the modern basement, where there is a supermarket -- the locals buy their groceries here *(www.mercatdesclaustre.com,* parking garage on the Plaça Miranda). Early risers should visit the INSIDER TIP fish market between Plaça del Carme and Plaça d'Espanya: everything from the sea is hawked very vocally *(Tue–Sat from 7.30am)*.

PLAÇA DE LA CONQUESTA (U B1) (∅ b1)

Here, in the oldest part of the town, is the cultural centre *Casa de Cultura* with an informative public library and the town archive; a few steps further on is the *town hall* (construction began in 1789). From the end of the short alleyway *Carrer d'Alfons III* you can enjoy a lovely INSIDER TIP panoramic view over the port.

PLAÇA DE S'ESPLANADA (U A2) (∅ a2)

From Plaça de S'Esplanada, *Carrer de ses Moreres* leads eastwards into the old part of the town. This is where the shopping district begins with boutiques, souvenir shops, pubs and restaurants and a bronze bust representing Dr Mateu Orfila (1787–1853), an illustrious resident of Maó. He is considered the founder of toxicology, the study of poisons, and was celebrated as one of the leading scientists of his time at the Institut Pasteur in Paris. At the end of the boulevard, *Carrer Bastió* forks off to the left, and if you go to the right it leads to *Costa d'en Deia* and *Plaça Reial* with the town's theatre, the *Teatro Principal*. Facing straight ahead, you would be looking at the town gate through which Barbarossa once forced his way into Maó before subjugating and plundering the town and abducting more than 1000 inhabitants. A dramatic footnote: a very small number of the merchants are said to have opened the gate for the pirates in order to protect their own property. From the Plaça heading north you come to the capital's bus station.

SANTA MARIA ★ (U B1) (∅ b1)

Construction of the Santa Maria parish church was started in 1748 on the ruins of an older chapel. Rather simple at first glance, Santa Maria appeals more to the ear than the eye because inside is a INSIDER TIP masterpiece of

LOW BUDGET

In addition to the town tours for which there is a charge, Maó town council occasionally offers free tours. You can get the dates and times at the tourist office or on *tel. 9 71 36 98 00.*

You can surf the net for free in Maó's town libraries (see p. 38) and in the cultural centre *Ateneu de Menorca (Mon–Fri 10am–2pm | Rovellada de Dalt 25 | www.ateneumao.org).*

Contemporary cuisine in a relaxed setting: the Ses Forquilles ("the forks") restaurant

organ building. In 1809 a commission was placed with the German-Swiss organ builders Otter & Kyburz and the instrument was delivered to Menorca in just one year. With its 3120 pipes and four manuals it was soon well-known throughout the island, especially for its ability to imitate the human voice *(June–Oct Mon–Sat 1pm 30 min. organ concerts | admission 5 euros)*. You can marvel at the lovely instrument on almost all weekdays *(Mon–Fri 10am–12.30pm, 4pm–7pm, Sat 10am–12.30pm | admission to church 2 euros). Between Plaça de la Conquesta and Plaça de la Constitució*

SANT FRANCESC (U A1) *(ĵ a1)*

The people of Maó also call this church the "cathedral". It took almost a century to build (1719–92), which is reflected in the mix of architectural styles. Next to it is the former Franciscan convent *Sant Francesc* founded in 1439, today the *Museu de Menorca*. The road there is lined with stately buildings. *Plaça des Monestir*

FOOD & DRINK

ARS CAFÉ ● (U C2) *(ĵ c2)*

This is a cosy café on the ground floor of a stately old sandstone house, furnished in a homely style and with Thonet chairs and bistro tables set against burgundy red walls. It is mostly locals who come here to enjoy good wines and, at lunchtimes and in the evenings, the good food too. In the *La Cava* cellar vaults you can enjoy jazz sessions *(from 11.30pm). Mon–Thu 9am–midnight, Fri/Sat 9am–4am | Plaça Princep 12 | tel. 9 71 35 18 79 | arscafe.wordpress.com/el-cafe | Moderate*

BAIXAMAR (U A1) *(ĵ a1)*

Modernismo (Spanish Art Nouveau) is the theme of this quayside café with its black and white tiles, dark wooden furniture and illuminating mirrors. Every generation and class of people meet up here at all times of the day and night in Maó. *Daily from 9am | Moll de Ponent 17 | www. cafebaixamar.es | Budget*

MERCAT DE PESCADOS
(U B–C2) *(ₘ b–c2)*

In a central location yet off the beaten track, this fish market sells everything the sea has to offer. Walking past the fish, you'll come around the other side of the market with a line of tapas bars displaying authentic Menorcan dishes such as mussels caught in the fjord, sausages and cheeses produced inland and delicate sweet pastries. *Mon–Sat 11.30am–3pm, 7.30pm–11pm | between Plaça del Carme and Plaça d'Espanya | Budget–Moderate*

NAUTIC LOUNGE (U E1) *(ₘ e1)*

A truly unique culinary experience! Take a seat in a small round boat with a BBQ built up in the centre and sail around and explore the harbour while your food is cooking on the grill (no yachting licence required). There are different menus to choose from, ranging from BBQ to sushi. *Starts 11.45am and 6.45pm | 300 Moll de Llevant | mobile 6 09 30 04 59 | www.nau ticlounge.com | Expensive*

RESTAURANTE PIZZERÍA ROMA
(O) *(ₘ O)*

This is probably Maó's most popular pizzeria, with reasonable prices, impeccable view of the port and an international ambience. Its lunchtime and evening menus (the latter only served off season) offer a variety of dishes: just ask Señor Enric what he recommends. *Moll de Llevant 295 | tel. 9 71 35 37 77 | www.res taurantepizzeriaroma.com | Budget–Moderate*

SES FORQUILLES (U A2) *(ₘ a2)*

Oriol and Raquel's young team serve tasty, nicely presented dishes with a creative

BOOKS & FILMS

The Life of Richard Kane – by Bruce Laurie, a serious academic study of Britain's first governor of Menorca presents a fascinating picture of life on the island in the 18th century, only available in hardback.

Brief summary to the History of Menorca – by Fernando Marti Camps, translated with adaptations for the English reader by Bruce Laurie, a bit idiosyncratic but interesting and well illustrated.

The Birds of Menorca – by Enric Ramos, this provides a description of all the species of birds to be found on Menorca. It is easy to use, is full of illustrations and a very practical guide.

Plants of the Balearic Islands – by Anthony Bonner, this indispensable pocket guide to the marvellous flora of the islands is now available in an excellent new edition. For the non-expert, it is ideal if you simply want to know what you are looking at as you stroll through the countryside.

Walk! Menorca – by David and Ros Brawn, a comprehensive guide to walks in Menorca with ratings for distance, time etc. There are clear maps and photos. But buy it before you go because it is not available in Menorca!

touch. Their speciality is Menorcan king prawns with smoke and truffles. Also tapas in a lively bistro atmosphere. *Closed Tue and Wed evenings and Sun | Rovellada de Dalt 20 | tel. 9 71 35 27 11 | www.sesfor quilles.com | Moderate*

SHOPPING

Carrer Hannóver (U B2) *(🗺 b2)* or – as the Menorcans prefer – *Costa de Sa Plaça*, is Maó's shopping street, dotted with small bars, here you can pick up books, clothing, souvenirs, hamburgers, shoes and more. *Plaça Colon* also offers something different with its palm trees and stone paving. This and *Carrer Nou* are the places to meet for a celebration or maybe just a cup of coffee. A lovely *market* (including arts and crafts) is held on *Tue and Sat 9am–2pm* on *Plaça de S'Esplanada* (U A2) *(🗺 a2)*. You should also pay a visit to the lively, well stocked market hall *Mercat del Claustre del Carme* (U C2) *(🗺 c2)* *(Mon–Sat 8am–9pm)*.

S'ALAMBIC
(U B1) *(🗺 b1)*
You can buy typical Menorcan souvenirs here in a typical Menorcan building: ceramics, costume jewellery, clothing, leather goods, liqueurs, wine, gin, cheese, honey and lots more. *Moll de Ponent 36*

DESTILERÍA GIN XORIGUER
(U A1) *(🗺 a1)*
You can get Gin Xoriguer in almost every bar and restaurant in Menorca. But here in Maós port is where it is produced and can be sampled. You can buy it in decorative glass or clay bottles. Try the herbal liqueurs, too! To this very day the Pons family keeps the secret of the key ingredients under lock and key.

Around 60 per cent of production is consumed on the island as *pomada* or neat. *Andén de Poniente 91 (branch in the old town: Plaça del Carme 16) | www.xoriguer.es*

HERMANOS LORA BUZÓN
(U A1) *(🗺 a1)*
Here the whole family is dedicated to the manufacture of hand-painted ceramics with rural motifs. You can also have a look in the workshop. *Moll de Ponent 8–10*

JAIME MASCARÓ (U A2) *(🗺 a2)*
Well-known shoe brands, all made locally, with unusual styles; they also sell belts and bags. *C/ Ses Moreres 29 | www.jaimemascaro.es*

LA MARVILLA (U B1–2) *(🗺 b1–2)*
Nice, small gift shop in the centre. They have something rather special: the friendly looking Menorcan mule neighing out at you from cups, aprons and T-shirts. *C/ Portal del Mar 7*

EL PALADAR (O) *(🗺 O)*
Finest quality Menorcan produce: cheese, ham, cold meats, pies, wine, cava etc. They also have a shop in Ciutadella and you can shop online: *www.elpaladar.es. C/ Ciutadella 97 | 250 m/273 yds from the town entrance*

PONS QUINTANA (U B2) *(🗺 b2)*
Here you will find some rather wacky women's shoes: from pink pumps to turquoise cowboy boots. *C/ S'Arravaleta 21 | www.ponsquintana.com*

SUCRERÍA CA'N VALLÉS (U B2) *(🗺 b2)*
This is where the connoisseurs reckon you can get the best *ensaïmadas* in town, also other tasty dishes typical of the island. *C/ Hannóver 16*

EL TURRONERO
(U B2) (*b2*)

If you are looking for edible Menorcan souvenirs, then you have struck gold here. The range of products includes not only sweets *(turrones)* and excellent ice cream, but also cheese and cold meats. *C/ Nou 22–24*

amarans.com) and the ship "Don Joan" by *Líneas de la Cruz (tickets: tel. 9 71 35 07 78 | rutasmaritimasdelacruz. com).* Both have underwater windows and the English commentary is clear and informative. *Líneas de la Cruz* also organises excursions to remote bays and beaches, some of which are otherwise inacces-

Wide range of vegetables at the Mercat del Claustre del Carme

VIDRIERIA BONAIRE (U B1) (*b1*)

If you have a weakness for hand cut glass, then this is the place for you: animal miniatures, glasses, bowls, mirrors. *C/ Sant Ciril 26 | www.vidrieriabonaire.com*

SPORTS & ACTIVITIES

BOAT TRIPS

The one-hour ⭐ *port cruise in Maó* focuses on Port de Maó and is a must for every holidaymaker on Menorca. Get an early start to avoid the crowds! Boats depart daily in summer from the port steps (close to the ferry terminal). Choose between the yellow boats *(Yellow Catamarans | reservations: mobile tel. 6 39 67 63 51 | www.yellocwat*

sible. Tours start from Maó and head north-east via Sa Mesquida to Illa d'en Colom and the Es Grau Nature Reserve as well as south via Punta Prima and Binibèquer to Canutells, with breaks for a swim in summer *(in summer daily 10am and 2.30pm, return approx. 1pm or 5.30pm).*

SAILING

From these companies in Maó you can book sailing trips and hire boats: *Menorca Náutica (Moll de Llevant 163 | tel. 9 71 35 45 43 | www.menorcanautic.com), Blue Mediterraneum (Moll de Llevant | mobile tel. 6 09 30 52 14), Menorca Cruising School (CMoll de Levant 303 | Sant Lluis | www.menorcasailing.co.uk | also sailing lessons)*

MAÓ

TENNIS

Club Tenis Mahón (C/ Trepucó 4 | tel. 9 71 36 05 76) (tennis court, floodlit).

ENTERTAINMENT

There are lots of things also for young people to do in the western port area around *Moll de Ponent* – bars, cafés and pubs that all cater for night owls. The ones most popular with locals are the cosy *Baixamar* (see "Food & Drink") and the jazz and dance club *Akelarre (Thu often live performances | Moll de Ponent 42 | www.facebook.com/akelarrejazzdance)* with cocktails and trendy clientele.

The eastern port district round *Moll de Llevant* has a more sedate and international feel. One institution is *Bar Nou (C/ Nou 1).* Housed in an art nouveau building in the upper part of the city close to the Santa Maria church, this bar serves cocktails in a quiet, vintage setting with a pretty outside seating area. Nightlife in Maó can also be found in *Assukar (Sun–Thurs from 8pm, Fri/Sat from 10pm | C/ Francesc Borja Moll)* which plays salsa and other Latin beats. A mix of theme parties, DJ sessions and live concerts is held at this venue and its terrace is a good place to enjoy a refreshing drink to cool down. If you're looking for somewhere quieter, head to the cellar bar *La Cava* in the warm and relaxing *Ars Café (Plaça Princep 12, see Food & Drink):* This former wine cellar has been transformed into a stylish nightspot with live music and DJ sessions. On the edge of the old town is the *Cristianal i Gradinata (C/ Isabel II.)* bar with fantastic views over the city and where Señor Chiqi has a preference for jazz and blues: the INSIDER TIP *Mirador des ses Monges* is just a few steps away where the city's harbour spreads out below you. This is a popular meeting point for locals. If you're looking for something in the way of culture, don't miss out on a concert at the ● *Teatre (Costa Deia 40 | www.teatremao.com)* Spain's oldest opera house offers amazing architecture and acoustics.

A must for fans of classic: a concert in Maó's theatre house

WHERE TO STAY

INSIDER TIP CASA ALBERTI ⚡
(U B2) (*m b2*)
Feel at home in this noble palace dating from 1740. Situated in one of the prettiest corners of the old town, climb the hotel's marble staircase to the spacious, high-ceilinged rooms, which are all furnished with antique furniture. Breakfast emphasises local produce and offers the perfect start to your day. Señora Blanca welcomes her guests like she would her friends. There is even an honesty fridge in the bar where guests can help themselves during the day (and write down what they have spent). The rooftop terrace offers a panoramic view of the region around. *7 rooms | C/ Isabel II. 9 | tel. 6 86 39 35 69 | www.casalberti.com | Moderate*

JARDI DE SES BRUIXES
(U C2) (*m c2*)
Originally dating from 1812, this old-town hotel was restored 100 years later in Art Nouveau style. The rooms at Ses Bruixes are individually decorated, each one with its own charm and original architectural features and modern bathrooms (free WiFi, fireplace). The continental breakfast is served in the romantic courtyard café – *al estilo menorquín* on request. *7 rooms | C/ de Sant Ferrán 26 | Tel. 9 71 36 31 66 | www.hotelsesbruixes. com | Moderate*

PORT MAHÓN ⚡ (0) (*m 0*)
The island capital's most prestigious hotel, a four-star establishment offering fantastic views over the sea and the marina. It is fully renovated and sumptuously furnished, with air conditioning, swimming pool and mini bar. *82 rooms | Av. Port de Maó 13 | tel. 9 71 36 26 00 | www.sethotels.com | Expensive*

RESIDENCIA JUME (U C2) (*m c2*)
You can stay here without spending a great deal of money. It offers modest comfort, decent accommodation and it is where lots of young visitors from the Spanish mainland come and stay. *39 rooms | C/ Concepció 4–6 | tel. 9 71 36 32 66 | www.hostaljume.com | Budget*

INFORMATION

OFICINA D'INFORMACIÓ TURÍSTICA
(U B2) (*m b2*)
Plaça Constitució 22 | town hall | tel. 9 71 36 37 90 | www.menorca.es | branch at the harbour: Moll de Llevant 2 | tel. 9 71 35 59 52

BUSES

Several times daily to Ciutadella *(bus station Pl. de S'Esplanada)*; information: *mobile tel. 9 71 36 04 75* (in Spanish) or at the tourist information. There are other regular connections from Maó to Es Castell, Sant Lluís, Es Migjorn Gran and Sant Tomàs, Ferreries and Cala Galdana, Sant Climent and Cala En Porter, to Alaior and Son Bou, Fornells and Arenal d'en Castell.

WHERE TO GO

ILLA DEL REI (131 E4) (*m J–K6*)
Governor Kane commissioned the construction of the huge hospital complex which to this day covers a major part of the small island in the Port de Maó bay. Since its construction in the 18th century until the 1950s, the building was used as a hospital. The island, which British seafarers 200 years ago christened *Bloody Island,* is shrouded in dark tales, and surgical waste is said to have been thrown into the sea in days gone by. In 1986 the Maó town council announced the build-

ing was to be used to establish a public institution and there was talk of a genetic research centre and of a museum; Elton John wanted to take up residence there; the Balearic Electricity Works wanted to establish a research facility; and speculators wanted to build a hotel. But to this day the building still stands empty. The remains of an early Christian basilica are to be found on Illa del Rei, though its main attraction, a relatively well preserved mosaic, is exhibited in the *Museu de Menorca* in Maó. The small island owes its name to Alfonso III of Aragon who landed there in 1287 and held out until reinforcements arrived to re-take Menorca from the hands of the Moorish occupying forces. *Visit April–Sept only Sun 8.45am with the "Yellow Submarine" | 5 euros | www.islahospital menorca.org*

LA MOLA ☆ (131 F4) *(∅ K6)*

Both the French and British occupiers of the island considered transforming the strategically important peninsula at the entrance to the bay of Maó into a bastion. However, the present fortress complex was constructed from 1850–60, after the demolition of the castle of San Felipe by the Spaniards. On the occasion of an inauguration, Queen Isabella II of Bourbon visited the fort, which was subsequently given the name "Fortalesa Isabel II". In 1930 the facilities were once again upgraded and two Vickers Armstrong guns were installed. However, the fortress was never involved in military conflicts, which is why it is so perfectly preserved and offers a variety of activities under the auspices of a Menorcan association. The activities include guided tours *(6 euros)*, bike rides, jeep safaris *(14.50 euros)* as well as concerts and theatre and dance performances. You will find the current events calendar at: *www.fortalesalamola.*

com. Access via Port de Maó, Carretera La Mola, 7 km/5 miles | May 10am–8pm, June–Sept 10am–8pm, Oct–April 10am–2pm | admission 8 euros

SA MESQUIDA (131 E3) *(∅ J–K5)*

This is where the people of Maó come to swim and sunbathe. The 700 m/765 yds coastline is divided into two parts by a headland. The larger beach is around 300 m/328 yds long, but is not well suited for children as the ground falls away quite steeply. Sa Mesquida was also the starting point in 1781 of the Franco-Spanish reconquest, which gave the British reason enough to secure the bay with its own fortification (1798). Restaurant tip: *Cap Roig (April–Oct | C/ de Sa Mesquida 13 | tel. 9 71 18 83 83 | www.restaurantcaproig. com | Budget–Moderate)*, inviting terrace overlooking the sea.

TALAIOT DE TREPUCÓ (131 E4) *(∅ J6)*

The prehistoric settlement situated 2 km/ 1.2 mile south of Maó is often described as the site with the most spectacular megalith in the Balearics, the *taula* (more than 4.20 m/13 ft high), and with the largest *talaiot* construction (40 m/131 ft diameter). Six more stone towers mentioned in ancient chronicles have now disappeared, perhaps having been used as building material for the barricades and ramps which the French Governor had built in 1781 so that he could fire from here at the Sant Felip fortress. *Admission free*

TALATÍ DE DALT (131 D4) *(∅ H6)*

This well preserved and restored ancient settlement was inhabited until the time of the Roman occupation. The stone pillar supporting the huge cap stone of the *taula* is quite striking. Access is signposted (main road Maó–Ciutadella, 4 km/2.5 miles). *10am–sunset | admission 4 euros | www.disfrutamenorca.com/talati-de-dalt*

Prehistoric settlement ruins near Maó: Talatí de Dalt

SANT CLIMENT

(131 D4) *(∅ H6)* **This has become the preferred place for the middle classes of Maó to retreat to where, hardly 10 km/6 miles from the island capital, one feels out in the country.**

You should have a look at the *Basílica des Fornas de Torelló* with a mosaic dating from the 6th century and the *Talaiot de Torelló* (both to the left of the Sant Climent–Maó main road, just before the turn off to the airport). The remarkable *Curnia* estate with elements of art nouveau is not far away; it is said to have been designed by a pupil of Gaudí. There is another *talaiot (Talaiot de Curnia | 2.8k m/1.7 mile)* behind the main building.

FOOD & DRINK

ES MOLÍ DE FOC

Good international cuisine with French influences in a pleasant atmosphere in the restored mill. In-house brewery. *C/ Sant Llorenç 65 | tel. 9 71 15 32 22 | www.es molidefoc.es | Moderate*

SHOPPING

You will find food and bakery products on the Sant Jaume thoroughfare, and Bernardo Pons' homemade cheese *(Quesos de Sant Climent)* in the C/ Sant Llorenç.

ENTERTAINMENT

INSIDER TIP RESTAURANTE CASINO SANT CLIMENT

Here you can enjoy an evening meal in a typical British atmosphere; there are jazz sessions on Tuesdays in summer from 8.30pm. *C/ Sant Jaume 4 | tel. 9 71 15 34 18 | www.casinosantcliment. com | Expensive*

WHERE TO GO

CALA EN PORTER
(130 B–C4) (*Ø G6*)

On the left (as you look from the sea) everything's still in a natural state, whereas on the right there is a holiday resort that extends up the slope. The beach at the end of the bay is 400 m/437 yds wide, with fine sand sloping down gently to the sea – ideal for the whole family. Be aware, however, that the word is out!

Disco with thrill factor: Cova d'en Xoroi

A first rate attraction is the nightclub with café ✹ *Cova d'en Xoroi (May–Sept daily 11.30am–9.30pm | admission inl. drink 8 euros | C/ de Sa Cova 2 | tel. 9 71 37 72 36 | www.covadenxoroi.com)*in a natural grotto. Location, view and atmosphere are unique. Halfway between sea and sky, on the steep slopes of the coastal cliffs, it provides a breathtaking view of the sea.

No wonder that this place has become something of a legend. The Moor pirate Xoroi (the one-eared), who was left behind by his crew on the coast of Menorca after a raid, is said to have used it as a base. Word spread amongst the peasants that there was a bandit in hiding: one day hens were missing, the next day a pig. And then one day a beautiful young peasant girl disappeared. The peasants only discovered the thief's hiding place years later when, one winter's night, some snow had fallen on the fields and footprints led them to the cave. The armed peasants stormed the pirate's cave and he hurled himself into the sea. They found the young woman in the best of health and with three children... A few kilometres inland, the hotel **INSIDER TIP** *Torralbenc (22 rooms | Ctra. Maó–, km 10 | tel. 9 71 37 72 11 | www.torralbenc.com | Expensive)* is also an attraction: The estate sits on a hillside, surrounded by vineyards. The rooms are furnished with natural materials, and there is a lovely pool garden from where you can overlook the landscape and the sea. Creative Menorcan cuisine is served in the restaurant.

CALES COVES ★ ●
(130 B–C4) (*Ø G6*)

Where 3000 years ago the original inhabitants buried their dead, there lived a clan of latter day hippies until the middle of the 1990s. The place name (cave bays) is in the plural because the bay is divided into two areas of land, in one of which there is a freshwater spring; both are deep into the greyish brown rock. Well protected from the wind, the water in the bay is calm and crystal clear, but access via a gravel path is very uneven. A more enjoyable route is to follow the red-signposted GR-223 trail from Cala en Porter on foot *(Start at the Mirador; the hike takes approx. . 1:40 hr one way).*

The caves total about 100 and have a complex past. The oldest date from the 11th century BC and were used as burial sites. Up to the 4th century BC larger caves were dug into the limestone rock, often with a central supporting column, benches and niches, also used as burial sites. Even Roman traces have been found. Some of the caves were used for ritual purposes and seafarers – also buccaneers – and fishermen repeatedly used the bay as a shelter in rough seas.

ES CANUTELLS
(130 C5) *(⌘ G–H7)*

For the inhabitants of Sant Climent the bay is their town "port". Special features are the boat houses carved into the cliff and the small beach, which is accessible via a weathered staircase. In recent years a resort has developed above the bay extending deep into the interior; only the western edge of the bay has so far been largely spared. On the road from Sant Climent to Sant Lluís, you can still admire a lovely example of Menorcan hybrid architecture: the manor *Casat de Formet (Forma Vell)* from the 19th century impresses with its red facade and beautiful, terraced garden with fountains and other water features.

SANT LLUÍS

(131 E5) *(⌘ J7)* **The small town always looks as though it has just been freshly painted with everything spic and span. White dominates, the houses are mostly flat-roofed, and the narrow streets quiet, with just a few children playing in the park at the village entrance, in the shadow of the large windmill.**

The restored *mill (Mon–Sat 10am–1pm)* contains a modest folklore exhibition. The village has about 4700 inhabitants, many of them having escaped from Maó. A growing community of foreign residents have also settled in Sant Lluís which has French roots. Count Lannion, governor when the island was under French rule, founded the place on a flying visit in the 18th century, designing it with pencil and ruler with the result that the town's layout is geometrical. The church which gave the place its name was dedicated to the French King Louis IX, but was only completed under British rule.

FOOD & DRINK

INSIDER TIP **BODEGAS BINIFADET**
It's worth a stop at the edge of Sant Lluís for a spot of wine-tasting in the middle of the region's vineyards. Snacks are also served but if you'd like to savour the tranquil atmosphere for longer, take a seat on the restaurant's terrace. *April–Oct 11am–6pm (wine tastings several times a day), Nov–March 10am–3pm (wine tasting only at noon) | Cami De Ses Barraques | tel. 9 71 15 07 15 | www.binifadet.com*

PAN Y VINO
In this 200 years old country house, the sounds of live jazz occasionally accompany the creative meals. Patrick and Noelia ensure a lively atmosphere. *Camí*

de la Coixa 3 (Torret) | tel. 9 71 15 03 22 | www.panyvinomenorca.com | Expensive

SA PEDRERA D'ES PUJOL

You can eat in fine style in this typical country house near San Lluís – in summer you can also sit out on the surrounding terraces. Creative cuisine and a wide selection of wines are further plus points. *Camí des Pujol 14 | towards Punta Prima, km 6 | tel. 9 71 15 07 17 | www.sapedreradespujol.com | Expensive*

INSIDER TIP LA RUEDA

Cheap tapas and set menus – no wonder it is often packed here around noon. Simple furnishings, noisy, good vibes! *Closed Tue | C/ Sant Lluis 30 | tel. 9 71 15 03 49 | Moderate*

INSIDER TIP TABERNA EL CORSO

The "tavern of the Corse" is worth a detour towards the coast. They serve authentic, homemade Mediterranean/ Spanish dishes with generous portions – and the service is also spot on. The chef himself often comes to the table to make sure his guests are all quite satisfied. *Urbanització Cala Torret 68 | tel. 9 71 15 06 80 | Moderate–Expensive*

ENTERTAINMENT

The beachside *Bucaneros* is a great place to enjoy a cool beer under the shade of a bamboo parasol. Live music is performed every full moon at the divers' haunt *Bar Paupa (Cala Torret)*.

WHERE TO STAY

INSIDER TIP BINIARROCA COUNTRY HOTEL

Dating from the 18th century, this country house is owned by Sheelagh Ratliff, a former London designer. She has transformed the property into a stylish retreat and entertains guests by providing lots of tips! Attractive garden grounds with two pools and sheltered pergola; French-style cuisine is served in the romantic restaurant. *18 rooms | Camí Vell 57; 2 km/1.8 mile from Sant Lluís | tel. 9 71 15 00 59 | www.biniarroca.com | Moderate– Expensive*

INFORMATION

Town hall | C/ de Sant Lluís | tel. 9 71 15 09 50

WHERE TO GO

S'ALGAR (131 E5) *(◊ K7)*

This is the place to holiday! *Club S'Algar Diving (Passeig Marítin | tel. 9 71 15 06 01 | www.salgardiving.com)*, the water sports centre, offers almost every type of water sport: diving, windsurfing, sailing, waterskiing, water rides, paragliding etc. Here you can also hire diving equipment and sailing boats as well as get your sailing or diving certificates. The *S'Algar Hotel (106 rooms | tel. 9 71 15 17 00 | www.salgarhotels.com | Expensive)* enjoys a good reputation as a family hotel. It has no direct access to the beach but has a fantastic swimming pool with sea views, spa area, massage and beauty treatments. If you fancy peace and quiet in a natural setting, you can walk round the little cove *Cala Rafalet* to the north at a height of 15–30 m (50–100 ft).

BINIBÈQUER VELL ★
(131 D5) *(◊ H–J7)*

The main tourist attraction on the southeast coast of Menorca is reminiscent of a rabbit warren. However, the structures of the "typical fishing village" are recent, although the winding alleys and narrow cobbled streets were supposedly designed by fishing forefathers. Prior to the

Stunning backdrop in radiant white: Binibèquer Vell

start of the season, the complex sparkles in pristine white, the natural stone floors are polished, souvenir shops and bars start to display their offers in the windows. In peak season it gets rather crowded in the narrow nooks and crannies. You can enjoy tapas, fresh fish and excellent chocolate cake in the *Club Náutico (near Hotel Eden, right by the sea | Moderate)*; relaxed atmosphere and superb sunsets.

CALA D'ALCALFAR (131 E5) (*ⓜ K7*)
This is how all the fishing villages on the island once looked. Cala d'Alcalfar (or Alcaufar) is a simple village, mainly used by Menorcans, with white boat houses by the sea. A natural breakwater at the entrance to the cove ensures a calm sea. Hotel tip: *Xuroy (46 rooms | tel. 9 71 15 18 20 | www.xuroymenorca.com | Budget)* on the edge of the village. The beach hotel is satisfactory and provides holidays away from the madding crowd.

PUNTA PRIMA
(131 E6) (*ⓜ J7*)
Punta Prima has a wide beach of fine, white sand that gently drops down to the sea, making it reasonably popular. *Illa de l'Aire*, a small island with lighthouse, lies just off the coast. Two hotel tips: at the *Barceló Pueblo Menorca (Sant Lluís | www. barcelo.com | Expensive)* the emphasis is on families with children. For the younger guests there is an entertainment programme while parents can enjoy an elaborate ● spa area with jacuzzi, steam bath, sauna and hot stone massage. The five-star hotel *Insotel Punta Prima Prestige (52 rooms | C/ Mitjanera de Punta Prima | Sant Lluís | tel. 9 71 19 51 61 | www.inso-telhotelgroup.com | Expensive)* oozes class: beautifully tended gardens, exquisite rooms, appealing architecture and an exclusive spa area with adjacent beauty and fitness centre all satisfy the most stringent demands.

TRAMUNTANA

"The Tramuntana does not rest and does not forgive", says a Menorcan proverb, and when you see the bizarre shapes of the coastal cliffs – weathered by storm and spray over thousands of years – and the deformed pine trees bent by the northerly winds, you can immediately agree.

It also explains why hundreds of galleons and fishing boats have sunk in the course of history off the rugged coast between Punta Nati and Cap de Favàritx, and why the people on the north coast tend to be rather quiet and introspective, because the *Tramuntana* shapes not only rock and wood, but also the inhabitants. And so, from time immemorial, psychological influences have been ascribed to this occasionally stiff north wind, and re-

cently medical statistics have proven the link between the wind and a tendency towards depression. Nevertheless, some of Menorca's most beautiful, unspoilt and quietest natural beaches are here: Cala Tirant, Port d'Addaia, Arenal de Son Saura, Cala Pregonda, Na Macaret...

FORNELLS

(128 B–C2) *(⫿ G2)* Here even the Spanish royal family occasionally enjoys a *caldereta*, which is particularly well made in ⭐ Fornells. And the setting is perfect too: a lovely, quiet lagoon on the otherwise rugged northern coast with the old fishing port whose inhabit-

Rugged, green north: where the constant wind shapes both the landscape and the nature of the people

ants enjoy a reputation as the best lobster fishermen in the western Mediterranean.
In this context "best" doesn't only refer to the size of the catch – the superb seafood is grilled daily in all the local pubs or dropped into the clay pot – but also to their careful management of the *langosta*, because the fishing season is limited to between April and August. And a further feature which has left it's mark on Fornells (pop. 1000): in the 1960s the Norwegian artist Arnulf

Björndal settled in Fornells and opened the island's first art gallery in the town centre (today closed). Other artists followed, mainly Scandinavian and Spanish, resulting in an eclectic artistic community.
Fornells itself dates from back to the 17th century. When King Philip IV had a small fortress erected at the entrance to the bay in 1625, fishermen and their families as well as the accompanying priest soon settled in a row of houses. The fortress and the church were not able to resist

the march of time – the present church is much younger, dating from the 18th century.

SIGHTSEEING

SA TORRE DE FORNELLS

This is one of 164 defence towers which the British erected primarily as a defence against their French opponents in the

ask for one. Tasty fish dishes, good *calderetas*, efficient service. *C/ Escoles 31 | tel. 9 71 37 64 42 | Expensive*

ES PLA

They serve one of the best (and also the most expensive at 75 euros) *calderetas* on the island which you can enjoy overlooking the quiet lagoon. Other dishes, however, are often adapted to interna-

Surf school in Fornells: a good place for beginners

western Mediterranean. It is the most important defence tower on the island. A small multimedia show and the tower itself provide insights into the defence of an island. *Mid April–Oct Tue–Sun 11am–2pm, 5–8pm | admission 2.50 euros*

FOOD & DRINK

ES CRANC

"The Crab" is not located directly on the seafront but is still a popular destination. Ask about prices before ordering though as you will only be handed a menu if you

tional tastes. This establishment is getting old and the service isn't quite what you'd expect. There is also an affordable lunch menu. *Pasaje Es Plá | tel. 9 71 37 64 03 | Expensive*

ES PORT ●

This may not have as lofty a reputation as *Es Pla*, but for many the Menorcan lobster *caldereta* is simply more authentic at *Es Port*. Good desserts, efficient service. However, in midsummer it can get very hot and congested on the narrow terrace outside. *C/ Gumersindo Riera 5 | Paseo Marítimo | tel. 9 71 37 64 03 | Expensive*

SPORTS & ACTIVITIES

Although Fornells is not officially regarded as a marina, there are a few moorings and water, electricity and showers are also available. Information: *tel. 9 71 37 66 04*

AVENTURA NÀUTICA

Excursions to *Marina Norte,* the marine nature reserve to the west of Fornells, are subject to strict control. *Aventura Nàutica* provides a tour with modern high performance dinghies, including a break for snorkelling. The three-hour boat trip costs around 60 euros per person (incl. soft-drinks). *Av. Passeig Marítim 41 | tel. 6 89 02 28 86 | www.aventuranautica menorca.com*

CAREMA CLUB PLAYAS

Not actually situated in Fornells, but on the western side of *Punta Mala*, on *Cala Tirant*, this three-star apartment hotel offers a 200 m^2/2153 ft^2 water park – fun for the whole family *(daily 11am–5pm)*. *Urbanización Playas de Fornells | Cala Tirant | tel. 9 71 15 42 18 | www.grupocar ema.com*

DIVING CENTER FORNELLS

The centre organises interesting dives on the north coast and also offers diving lessons. *Passeig Marítim 68 | tel. 9 71 37 64 31 | mobile 6 19 41 41 51 | www.diving fornells.com*

SERVINÀUTIC MENORCA

Motor and sailing boat hire, waterskiing, and also sailing courses are available. *C/ Major 27 | mobile tel. 6 29 27 32 09 | www. menorcaservinautic.com*

WIND FORNELLS

Here you can be taught by professionals to sail and surf; later you can also hire surfboards, small dinghies and catama-

rans. *At the port | mobile tel. 6 64 33 58 01 | www.windfornells.com*

ENTERTAINMENT

Well-heeled visitors to Menorca appreciate the evening stroll along the promenade; most tables in the restaurants are reserved in anticipation.

BAR SA TAULA

This is the place to chill out over a cocktail and enjoy the sea view. The roof terrace provides a really magical atmosphere at

---

★ **Fornells**
The charm of the old fishing port on a delightful lagoon contrasts with the otherwise rugged north coast
→ p. 52

★ **S'Albufera des Grau**
More than 90 bird species inhabit the second largest wetlands in the Balearics
→ p. 56

★ **Cap de Cavalleria**
Rugged northern cape with lighthouse and spectacular views → p. 57

★ **Cap de Favàritx**
This section of coast is ideal for those seeking unspoilt nature and peace and quiet
→ p. 57

★ **Monte Toro**
Magnificent views from the highest peak on the island – and meals in the convent restaurant → p. 59

MARCO POLO HIGHLIGHTS

sunset. The design of the building (and its name) is based on the island's prehistoric landmark. *C/ Major 1*

WHERE TO STAY

HOSTAL PORT FORNELLS ☆
The small, family-run hotel boasts a stunning view over the bay at Fornells. It has peaceful, sunny terraces, is surrounded by greenery and lies just outside the town. Rental cars and bikes are available for excursions. Free WiFi. *23 rooms | C/ des Port Fornells | Urb. Ses Salines (approx. 1 km/0.6 mile from Fornells) | tel. 9 71 37 63 73 | www.hostalportfornells. com | Moderate*

INSIDERTIP LA PALMA
This offers basic accommodation and is adjacent to a fishermen's pub. If you are keen on reasonable prices and a natural atmosphere, then this is the place. *23 rooms | Pl. de S'Algaret 3 | tel. 9 71 37 66 34 | www.hostallapalma.com | Budget*

INFORMATION

OFICINA D'INFORMACIÓ TURÍSTICA
C/ Major, 57 | tel. 9 71 15 84 30 | www.ajes mercadal.org | only in the summer

WHERE TO GO

S'ALBUFERA D'ES GRAU ★ ◎
(129 D–E 3–5) (*∅ H–J 3–5*)
As justification for the island becoming a *Reserva de la Biosfera*, the second largest wetland in the Balearics – the largest is the Albufera Gran on Mallorca – was used as the centrepiece. In 1995 the island's government honoured its promise to declare the area, measuring 4500 acres, a nature reserve. In fact Albufera d'Es Grau only just escaped "death by development". At the start of the 1970s the *Shangri-La* holiday resort was built on the eastern banks of the lagoon and it was only massive protests by the population that brought the project, already under construction, to a halt.

Coastline in the S'Albufera des Grau nature reserve

Today more than 90 bird species, including osprey, cormorants and heron, breed on the edge of the shallow waters. The salt water lagoon itself covers 165 acres and is populated by eels and turtles. The protective measures in the Albufera include a ban on driving, a prohibition on camping (also for campervans), a ban on making fires and a ban on all forms of water and motor sport. Hiking is, however, permitted. At the entrance to *Es Grau* there is a small building where you can pick up information and maps of the area; this is also where guided hikes start from (see also "Discovery Tours, p. 99). In 2003 the reserve was extended to 8550 acres; the ocean's edge in front was also declared a protected area. A larger information centre has also been set up: *Centre de Recepció Rodríguez Femenias (April–Oct Tue–Thu 9am–7pm, Fri–Sun 9am–3pm, Nov–March Tue–Thu 9am–5pm, Fri–Sun 9am–3pm | admission free | Ctra. Maó–Es Grau, Me-9, km 3.5, turnoff "Llimpa" | southeast of Fornells | tel. 9 71 17 77 05).*

CALA BINIMEL-LÀ (128 A2) (*ሀ F2*)

This bay is not quite as quiet as the neighboring bay *Cala Pregonda* (which can be reached via a coastal path) but is nonetheless attractive with its red, rather coarse sand and a small freshwater spring; there is also a small bar-restaurant.

CALA TIRANT (128 B2) (*ሀ F2–3*)

Just before you enter Fornells a road branches off to the left to a holiday resort which has spread over the steep cliffs at Cala Tirant. The beach is wide but is often strewn with seaweed.

CALA DE SA TORRETA (129 E4) (*ሀ J4*)

The bay (3 km/2 miles north of Es Grau) is not easily accessible and therefore not much frequented. It owes its name to an old watchtower. There is a small sandy beach and a ☙ lovely view of *Illa d'en Colom*.

CAP DE CAVALLERIA ★ ☙
(128 B1) (*ሀ F2*)

The view from around the lighthouse, which stands proudly on this northern cape, is simply stunning. To the left, over massive drops, you can see the rocky island *Illa des Porros*, to the right, the *Cap de Fornells*; towards the north, the view extends far over the sea to the horizon, towards the south to the deeply indented *Cala Tirant* bay and inland to *Monte Toro*, Menorca's highest mountain. The access to the cape through the windswept landscape is fun; you might come across wild goats. The *Santa Teresa* estate once housed the the the *Ecomuseu de Cap de Cavalleria* with exhibits tracing the history of the Roman settlement Ciutat Romana de Sanitja. Then the estate owner cancelled the tenancy, and the museum is supposed to move into the lighthouse. But many years might pass until then... West of the cape you can find fantastic beaches: The wild, romantic *Platja de Cavalleria* (or Ferragut), the *Cala Binimel·là* and the *Cala Pregonda* are connected to the hiking path *Camí de Cavalls* (see also "Discovery Tours", p. 98/99).

CAP DE FAVÀRITX ★ ☙
(129 E3) (*ሀ J3–4*)

A lighthouse — with striking black and white horizontal bands – bizarre black shale rock formations and its utter isolation characterise this cape, offering fabulous views of the sea and north-east coast.

COVA POLIDA (128 C2) (*ሀ G2*)

The cave is only accessible from the water and only when the sea is calm, but it is rich in stalactite formations.

ES GRAU (129 E4) *(ᗑ J4–5)*

The small fishing port (32 km/20 miles southeast of Fornells) is becoming a more and more popular destination for Menorcans and the narrow street and port bars are very busy, especially at weekends. Fine grey sand, a gently sloping beach, protected from the wind and waves by the island of Colom, and its almost perfect semi-circular shape are the features that define Platja d'Es Grau beach. However, in summer the bay throngs with pleasure crafts. You can go on an excursion and take a course on a single or two seater kayak with *Menorca en Kayak (C/ S'Arribada 8 | www.menorcaenkayak.com)*. Once you have done the course you can also hire boats and set off on your own.

ILLA D'EN COLOM ● (129 E4) *(ᗑ J4)*

In summer a pleasure boat *(departure from the port in Es Grau, Moll d'es Magatzems | four times daily)* makes the 500 m/547 yds crossing. There are two sandy beaches where you can enjoy a swim, but the island itself is pathless and rugged. The remains of an British quarantine hospital and a basilica are buried beneath undergrowth, waiting to be uncovered.

ES MERCADAL

(128 B3–4) *(ᗑ F4)* **The predilection of the people of Mercadal for bright, brilliant colours is striking, especially in contrast to the dark tones in the neighbouring town of Ferreries.**

Almost all the buildings are painted white, the streets usually wide and pleasant. But above all the town (pop. 5400) holds culinary promise to Menorcans as first communions, weddings and other family celebrations are given pride of place in the restaurants. Es Mercadal is also well-known for the production of cakes and pastries. Shoes are also made here, *avarques*, which are typical of Menorca, with soles made of tyre rubber and rawhide uppers.

FOOD & DRINK

MOLÍ DES RACÓ

In spite of its simple furnishings this is a good tip for those wanting to enjoy authentic Menorcan cuisine, in a lovely, 300 year old mill with a nice, relaxed ambience. *C/ Major 53| tel. 9 71 37 53 92 | www.restau rantemolidesraco.com | Moderate*

TAST RESTAURANTE

The restaurant in the town centre also enjoys an excellent reputation with the locals. It offers a wide range of tapas, a cultured ambience and an interesting mixture of traditional Menorcan and modern creative cuisine. *Plaça Pare Camps 21| tel. 9 71 37 55 87 | www.tastmercadal.com | Moderate*

The old convent on Monte Toro has a pretty courtyard

SHOPPING

The market *(C/ Nou)* is open *Sun 11am–2pm* in the summer. Every Thursday you can meet the artisans at the *Mercat Artesanal (7pm–10pm, in winter 6.30pm–9.30pm | Plaça del Pare Camps)*. A folklore group plays music to dance to. The INSIDER TIP *avarques* workshop *(Taller Gabriel Servera)* can be found in *Carrer Metges Camps 3*. The well-known confectioner *Cas Sucrer (Sa Plaça)* produces excellent quality *turrón* (which can be marzipan, ground peanuts, Turkish honey or chocolate) and *amargos* (almond paste). The *Centre Artesanal de Menorca (see p. 108)* at Carrer Metge Camps exhibits and sells regional arts and crafts – every item is unique.

WHERE TO STAY

JENI

This guesthouse in the town centre is more suited for a flying visit to the Es Mercadal area than a long stay. The rooms are basic but clean and there is a small swimming pool in the garden, and the food is appreciated not only by guests. *36 rooms | Mirada del Toro 81 | tel. 9 71 37 50 59 | www.hostaljeni.com | Moderate*

WHERE TO GO

MONTE TORO ★
(128 B4) (*m G4*)

Like a hedgehog with antennae and spines, the 357 m/1230 ft Monte Toro *(El Toro)* rises up out of the slightly hilly landscape. The island's highest elevation offers not only a fantastic panoramic view of Tramuntana to the north and Migjorn to the south, but is also a point of orientation for the fishermen at sea, and also provides wide areas of Menorca with good radio and TV reception. At the eastern entrance of Es Mercadal an access road branches off to Monte Toro. Today it is mainly holidaymakers who make the pilgrimage to the *Monte*, the nickname the Menorcans know the mountain by. The 17th century *Mare de Deu del Toro* chapel nestles in the shadow of the transmitter masts. It is from here that the bishop gives the island his blessing in May. The Madonna is the patron saint of Menorca. In a vault next to the chapel, Franciscan nuns sell religious souvenirs, books and postcards. The **INSIDER TIP** convent restaurant *Sa Posada del Toro (only during the day | tel. 9 71 37 51 74 | www. saposadadeltoro.com | Budget)* serves good Menorcan food, generous portions and an affordable lunch menu. *Sa Roca de S'Indio*, the "Indian's head" carved by nature into the rock, is rather less spectacular than its fame would suggest; it can be seen from the main Es Mercadal–Maó road on the right hand side, immediately beyond Es Mercadal (128 B4) (*ω F4*).

PORT D'ADDAIA

(129 D3) (*ω H3*) **The bay winds its way deep into the interior rather like a river, thus providing natural protection to one of the few harbours on Menorca's north coast.**

The slopes of the inlet are covered with evergreen bushes and the landscape seems quiet and sleepy. The unobtrusive buildings of the holiday resort are harmoniously integrated into the landscape. And yet not many miles further east (towards Cap de Favàritx) the coast has black shale that has been shaped over millennia by the wind and sea into bizarre shapes. The *Bistro Bar El Castillo* is always popular.

FOOD & DRINK

RESTAURANTE ADDAIA
This restaurant serves an unusually wide range of food from pizza to lobster flambé with Calvados. *Av. Port d'Addaia, L-2 | town entrance | tel. 9 71 35 92 61 | Moderate*

SPORTS & ACTIVITIES

CLUB NÀUTICO D'ADDAIA
Small, well-kept marina on the eastern side of Cala Molí, with 150 moorings but no fuel pumps. *Puerto Deportivo Addaia | tel. 9 71 18 88 71*

AMONGST VULTURES

You may spot a solitary bird circling high up in the sky at a leisurely pace. If you can make out a white body and dark wing tips then it may possibly be one of the rare *alimoches* (Egyptian vultures). This small species of vulture *(neóphron percnopterus)* lives individually, in pairs or in small groups in the quiet countryside and on the island's northern cliffs and does not migrate in the winter. The majestically soaring bird has become a symbolic creature on Menorca, embodying the spirit of the island and its unspoilt nature for the local inhabitants since time immemorial. See it on a guided bird-watching tour *(max. 6 people, 40 euros/pers. | menorcawalkingbirds.com).*

WHERE TO STAY

HOLIDAY HOMES

Rent a cosy villa by the sea? The dream can come true. Contact the agency: *Menurka Grup (C/ del Pilar 211 | 07740 Urb. Port d'Addaya | tel. 9 71 38 14 15 | www.menurka. com)*

SA TORRE BLANCA (129 D4) (*ⓜ J4*)

The successful dairy farmer rents out his tower: fine holiday accommodation for up to three people. And you can enjoy unspoilt countryside on the edge of the S'Albufera d'Es Grau nature reserve with a view of Cap de Favàritx. *On the road to Cape (C1) signposted | Post: Apdo. Correos 354 | 07780 Mahón | tel. 9 71 18 83 08 | www.satorreblanca.com | Moderate*

INFORMATION

Town hall in Es Mercadal | tel. 9 71 37 50 02 | www.aj-esmercadal.org

WHERE TO GO

ARENAL D'EN CASTELL
(128 C2–3) (*ⓜ H3*)

Modern holiday resort with one of the most beautiful beaches on the island that gently slopes down to crystal clear water. The *Castell Playa Fiesta (Closed Nov–April | 265 rooms | Platja d'En Castell | tel. 9 71 35 80 88 | www.palladiumhotelgroup. com | Expensive)* is a family hotel for the discerning guest. It has a sauna, swimming pool, jacuzzi and play area.

ARENAL DE SON SAURA
(128 C2) (*ⓜ G3*)

Small holiday resort with a clean, white, semicircular sandy beach around 300 feet long. There is a simple restaurant, waterskiing, surfing and pedalo hire. If you'd like a bit more peace and quiet,

Arenal d'en Castell: one of Menorca's most beautiful beaches

then you can take the path (about 1.2k km/0.75 mile) at the left end of the beach to the next small cove, *Cala Pudent*, where there are usually only a few bathers.

NA MACARET (129 D3) (*ⓜ H3*)

The small bay of *Cala Molí* is situated to the left on the same inlet as Port d'Addaia. As you drive out you will come to a fishing port and the Na Macaret holiday resort. The small port is today a base for fishermen working far out at sea.

SON PARC (128 C2) (*ⓜ G3*)

The first and, to date, only golf course on the island *(www.golfsonparc.com | see "Sports & Activities", p. 103)* is surrounded by a pine groves and a resurgent holiday resort.

MIGJORN/ ISLAND CENTRE

His Highness the Archduke Ludwig Salvator, with a deep and intimate knowledge of the Balearics and a sense for the environment already over a century ago, described the south of Menorca as rather unhealthy. He was especially suspicious of the *barrancs*, the ravines created over millennia where the rain eroded the soft limestone.

When it was very hot, the aristocrat claimed to have discerned "mephitic gases" there – foul-smelling fumes – which "encouraged malaria". The original inhabitants of the island, however, saw things differently because the soil is more fertile here and the climate manifestly more bearable than on the rugged north coast.

And most holidaymakers on Menorca, from today's perspective, would certainly deny the archduke's extravagant statements, because this is precisely where some of the most popular holiday destinations are situated: the magical bay of Cala Galdana, the long beaches at Sant Tomàs and Son Bou and the peaceful bathing bay at Cala Trebalúger.

The area is also of interest to amateur archaeologists. In and between the large *barrancs* in Menorca's south-west there are countless traces of prehistoric sites to explore. In every square mile you can find up to 60 archaeological sites, and remarkable concentration makes the island one of the richest centres for prehistoric finds in Europe.

Photo: Cala Mitjana

The delightful side of the island – the longest beaches, the most famous bays and the largest hotels are here in the south of the island

ALAIOR

(130 C3) (*ili G5*) **Picturesque white-washed houses stacked on the hilltop overlooked by a centrepiece church and small cobblestone streets just waiting to be explored; this is Menorca's unspoilt, authentic side away from the hordes of tourists! Alaior (pop. 9400) is the main town in the third largest municipality on the island and home to Menorca's university.**

Alaior is also regarded as synonymous with the island's famous cheese. The Coinga agriculture co-operative alone, who produces Menorcan cheese with the Queso Maó designation of origin, has a stock of over 10,000 dairy cows maintained by around 100 happy dairy farmers. Another well-known brand in the area is *La Payesa* and, until a few years ago, local milk was also used by *La Menorquina*, an up-market brand of ice cream very popular throughout the Balearics. In addition to cows and cheese, a shoe factory is managing to hold its head above water in Alaior (pronounced: *aló*), and costume jewellery is also produced here in family businesses.

The town was founded in 1304 and soon made a name for itself as a prosperous producer of woollen goods. Many of the leads you into its dimly lit interior where the gold-leaf Baroque altar will undoubtedly catch your eye. Alaior's third church, *Sant Pere Nou,* stands on the hillside and marks the spot close by for the start of the *Camí del Cos* horserace held every year to coincide with the town's patron saint cel-

Alaior: once famous for its woollen goods, but now for Menorcan cheese

older buildings date from the flourishing 17th century including the former Franciscan monastery *Sant Diego* from 1629, a white cube with clock tower, which today houses an exhibition centre. The adjacent monastery with cloister, *Pati de Sa Lluna,* serves as the town's tourist information in summer. Local art is exhibited in the town hall built in 1612 *(ajuntament)* and located on the main road through the town. The palace building opposite houses a school of the University of the Balearic Islands. The massive Baroque church of *Santa Eulària* is just a few feet away; its brown sandstone walls stand in stark contrast to the sea of white-washed houses around. A side entrance ebrations (on the 2nd weekend in August). Menorca's prettiest cemetery *(cementiri)* is worth the few minutes' walk: monumental mausoleums sheltered by cypresses, palm trees and bougainvillea.

FOOD & DRINK

BLAN BLAU
More a classic tapas bar than restaurant. But the little snacks are lovingly prepared and they also serve roast chicken, hamburgers and cocktails. *Daily 7am–midnight | C/ Es Carrero 38 | tel. 9 71 37 24 91 | www.blanciblautapasbar.com |* Budget

INSIDER TIP ▶ BRASSERIE & BAR DOS PABLOS

Some visitors may still remember the popular British restaurant, *Cobblers*. It relocated in 2014 and changed its name. The British owners dispel the myth of English cooking and conjure up new dishes every year to the delight of locals and tourists alike! *May–Oct daily from 6.30pm | C/ de la Mediterrània 3 | tel. 971377912 | www.facebook.com/brasseriebardospablos | Moderate–Expensive*

ES CORB MARI

This chill-out beach bar is a perfect place to relax and enjoy life, whatever the time of day or night. Why not finish your day in style with a well-shaken Mojito while watching the sunset over the island? Serves a wide range of cocktails, fresh seafood and fine desserts often accompanied by live music. *May–Oct daily from 10am | Playa de Son Bou, near the Hotel Melía Sol Milanos | tel. 609257924 | Moderate*

FORN DE TORRE SOLI NOU

Housed in a traditional Menorcan building with a spectacular terrace. But its interior is also spot on, the meat dishes excellent and the ice cream homemade. *Urb. Torre Soli Nou 28 | main road towards Son Bou | tel. 971372898 | www.esforntsn.com | Moderate*

GROKIBLAU

A meeting place for young people that is a relaxed mojito bar. They serve pizza, cheap and tasty *bocadillos* (sandwiches) and various salad dishes, and it has a chilled out "meditating Buddha" ambience. Very reasonable children's menu. *Ctra. Nova 112 | tel. 971378589 | Budget*

SHOPPING

From the end of June until September, there is an arts and crafts market (with tastings of regional specialities, folk music and workshops) in the centre on Wednesday evenings *(7–11pm)*. You can pick up classic ladies' and gentlemens' shoes at *Pons Quintana (Centre Comercial Balearica | C/ Sant Antoni 120 | www.ponsquintana.com)* and also very elegant shoes at the shoe factory *Gomila Melia S. A. (C/ Miguel de Cervantes 46 | www.gomila.es)*.

You can sample, and buy cheese at *Coniga (Ctra. Nova Parc 78 | www.coniga.com)* or at *La Payesa (Pons Martín | C/ Es Banyer 64 | www.lapayesa.es)*.

SPORTS & ACTIVITIES

SON BOU SCUBA

An expertly run diving school in the coastal resort of Son Bou. Courses are

---

⭐ **Basílica de Son Bou**
Menorca's most impressive example of an early Christian basilica → p. 66

⭐ **Torralba d'en Salort**
The most beautiful and best preserved *taula* on Menorca → p. 66

⭐ **Torre d'en Galmés**
A complete town was created from three *talaiots* and one *taula* sanctuary → p. 66

⭐ **Cala Galdana**
A picturesque bay: surrounded by dark grey coastal cliffs → p. 69

MARCO POLO HIGHLIGHTS

available for every level with regular diving excursions organised to offshore shipwrecks and caves. Diving equipment is also available for hire. *April–Oct | Centro Comercial San Jaime | mobile tel. 6 96 62 82 65 | www.sonbouscuba.com*

WHERE TO STAY

ROYAL SON BOU – FAMILY CLUB

Family friendly apartment hotel by the sea – just a few hundred feet away from Menorca's longest beach – with every comfort, in a flat-roofed building in the Menorcan style. *252 apartments | Platja de Son Bou | tel. 9 71 37 23 58 | www.royal sonbou.com | Moderate–Expensive*

SOL ELITE MILANOS PINGUÏNOS

With more than 1000 beds, this establishment in two tall buildings right on the beach is a real heavyweight amongst the island's hotels. It has a garden, swimming pool, tennis courts and entertainment for the youngsters. From the upper floors you can enjoy **INSIDER TIP** magnificent panoramic views of the sea and the dunes. *Platja de Son Bou 10 | tel. 9 71 37 12 00 | www.melia. com | Expensive*

CAMPING SON BOU

Clean campsite with pine forest and grassy areas. All the necessary services are on offer, and two types of accommodation can be booked so you can stay without camping equipment. *Ctra. de San Jaume, km 3.5 | tel. 9 71 37 27 27 | info and reservations at: www.campingsonbou. com*

INFORMATION

In the Franciscan monastery: Mon–Sat 10am–1.30pm, 5.30–9pm, Sun 4–9pm | tel. 9 71 37 83 22

WHERE TO GO

PLATGES DE SON BOU
(130 A–B 3–4) (*F5–6*)

With a length of 4 km/2.5 miles, the *Platges de Son Bou* is the longest sandy beach on Menorca. Fine, golden sand, a gentle slope down to the sea and showers and toilets make it ideal for families. For children there is a small playground in the adjacent *Sant Jaume* resort *(see "Travel with Kids", p. 108)*. In the 4th century a small village is said to have been situated on the eastern end of the beach (aerial photographs reveal a street grid in the sea), but today only the remains of the ★ *Basílica de Son Bou*, unearthed in 1951, are to be seen. They include the bases of two rows of columns dividing the main building into two narrower aisles, a wide nave, foundations and a large stone baptismal font with cloverleaf shaped bowl. The basilica, erected in the 5th century, gives the clearest indication of the architectural characteristics of the early Christian basilicas of Menorca.

TORRALBA D'EN SALORT ★
(130 C3) (*G5*)

This *talaiot* settlement from around 1000 BC, extended just a few years ago into an archaeological park, is situated on the secondary road from Alaior to Cala en Porter. The *Sa Taula de Torralba* sanctuary, one of the best preserved on the island, is quite outstanding. Animal bones and a small bronze bull statue were found in the area around the circle of megaliths.

TORRE D'EN GALMÉS ★ ●
(130 B3) (*G5–6*)

One of the most extensive areas of archaeological finds in the Balearics is situated 2.5 km/1.5 mile away on the main Alaior–Son Bou road. Three *talaiots* and a *taula* sanctuary must have formed a small town around 1400 BC, of which the remains of rooms, defensive walls, cisterns, caves and storage chambers are still to be seen. The burial chamber, situated a little beyond the other remains, (today known by the name of *Ses Roques Llises*) is also outstanding, as is a hall covered with stone blocks, *Sa Camera de sa Garita*, which was probably used as a storage or assembly room. *Admission 3 euros*

FERRERIES

(127 E4) (*ॐ E4*) With its rust-red cliffs, reddish brown fields and a new part of the town near the main road which is certainly not a thing of beauty, the town of Ferreries (pop. 4600), at first view, is rather off-putting.

However, an atmospheric old town in the upper area more than compensates for those first negative impressions. Carrer de Sa Font, especially, has nooks and crannies exuding an ancient charm, and the environmental museum *Centre de la Natura de Menorca (see "Travel with Kids", p. 108)* is also well worth seeing.

The name of the place conjures up thoughts of iron and early iron processing (the Latin word *ferrum* means iron). However, the town did not acquire any real significance until the road was built by Richard Kane, the respected British governor of the island, linking Maó and Ciutadella and establishing Ferreries in the island's trading network. European institutions once again came to the assistance of the town a few years ago: the region's products are now being supported and promoted with EU funds. The former market hall in the centre of the town, dating from the time of Franco, is worth seeing. It has been completely renovated and was reopened in 2011 and is now an architectural show-

The Festes de Sant Bartomeu are celebrated in Ferreries in August

piece which has won several awards. It is intended that the building be used primarily for cultural purposes.

FOOD & DRINK

RESTAURANTE LIORNA

An idiosyncratic mix of art and gastronomy with changing menus and exhibitions. The pizzas are recommended. If you are looking for a creative ambience and are willing to overlook serving errors, then this is the place for you. *Fri–Sun only, from 8pm | C/ Econòm Florit 9 | tel. 9 71 37 39 12 | Expensive*

SHOPPING

The Mercat de Nit, a popular Friday market in the centre *(July/Aug 7–11pm)*, sells fruit, vegetables, cold meat, cheese and other typical island specialities as well as arts and crafts. You really must try out the *bunyols de fromatge* in one of the bakeries in the old town. They are dough fritters fried in oil with a cheese filling and are a local speciality. The goldsmith *Núria Deyà (C/ Ciutadella 12a | tel. 9 71 37 35 23 | www. nuriadeya.com)* makes lovely jewellery with natural motifs and simple shapes in her small workshop.

CALZADOS RIA S.L.

This is where *avarques*, the typical Menorcan sandals, have been made since 1947. They have leather uppers and car tyre soles. There is a showroom next door. *C/ Goya 3–5 | tel. 9 71 37 30 70 | www.ria.es*

INSIDER TIP ▶ HORT DE SANT PATRICI ●

It's hard to think of a more appropriate setting to discover more about local cheeses and taste some too: set in Mediterranean gardens, this estate is located 1 km/0.6 mile to the north of Ferreries. While the manor house accommodates the *Ca Na Xini* hotel (see below), the former pigsties have been transformed into a cheese museum where visitors can find out how some of Spain's best dairy products are made. You also get the opportunity to taste the homemade dairy produce and wines at the end of the museum tour. The delicatessen sells honey, homemade jams and smoked sausage. *Camí de Sant Patrici | sale Mon–Sat 9am–1pm and 4–6pm, in the summer until 8pm, Sun 9am–1pm | admission 4.50 euros | tel. 9 71 37 37 02 | www.santpatrici.com*

ENTERTAINMENT

In summer you can watch demonstrations by the best Spanish riding school the *Club Escola Menorquina (June–Sept Wed and Sun from 8.30pm | Ctra. Ferreries–Cala* *Galdana, km 0.5 | reservations and info: tel. 9 71 37 34 97).*

WHERE TO STAY

CAMPING S'ATALAIA

S'Atalaia, one of the island's two official camp sites, is situated on the main Ferreries–Cala Galdana (km 4) road. It has good facilities, a swimming pool, clean showers and a small supermarket and is only about 3 km/2 miles from the sea. *Tel. 9 71 37 42 32 | www.campingsa talaia.com | Budget*

INSIDER TIP ▶ CA NA XINI ☺

Those who spend the night will not want to leave: set in romantic grounds, the villa's historic architecture and minimalistic design are sure to please as is the breakfast with homemade, organic specialities, served al fresco and accompanied by the sounds of birds singing. The hotel is connected to the *Hort de Sant Patrici* estate with dairy and bodega where you can acquaint yourself with traditional Menorcan cuisine. No children allowed! *8 rooms | Camí de Sant Patrici | tel. 9 71 37 45 12 | www.canaxini.com | Expensive*

SES SUCRERES

The sweets for the children of Ferreries were once made in this country manor house. Since 2010 they've been providing accommodation: simple, clean and in typical Menorcan ambience. You also get free homemade sweets. Six individually designed rooms. *Open all year | C/ Sant Joan 15 | tel. 9 71 37 41 92, mobile 6 44 26 02 27 | www.hotelsessucreres.com | Moderate*

SON TRIAY AGROTURISMO

On the same main road as the campsite (see above, turn off to the right) you come to this country B&B with a swimming pool and a tennis court. *14 rooms | tel. 9 71 15 50 78 | www.sontriay.com | Moderate*

INFORMATION

Town hall | Carrer de Sant Bartomeu 55 | tel. 9 71 37 30 03

WHERE TO GO

CALA GALDANA ⭐ (127 D5) (*∅ D5*)

This bay is especially popular with British, Spanish and German holidaymakers in search of their dream holiday. At one time this green oasis, surrounded by dark grey coastal cliffs, was described as "picturesque" or "like paradise". Unfortunately its charm is today being buried under concrete: the *Cala Galdana* resort is constantly expanding with new apartments, holiday flats, restaurants and supermarkets, especially into the western foothills of the bay. As you arrive, level with the first hotel (turn off to the left), you will gain a ⚡ good overview. The beach is a good 500 m/528 yds long with fine golden sand making it ideal for families with small children. The sea within the bay only becomes rough with a southerly wind, which is rare. The lovely *El Mirador (www.elmirador-restaurante.com | Expensive)* restaurant has a pleasant terrace and serves a wide range of grilled meat and fish and has a fantastic location on the peninsula.

Cala Galdana has numerous hotels so it is best, and certainly cheaper, to make your selection from home. But here are at least two tips: if you are on your own looking for a quiet holiday, the ⚡ *Hotel Audax Spa & Wellness (Urbanització Serpentiona | tel. 9 71 15 46 46 | www. artiemhotels.com | Expensive)* may not be going to be your first choice, but the modern hotel is a few hundred feet from the beach and overlooks the picturesque bay. It also has a large ● spa area. It caters mainly for a younger clientele, and there is free WiFi. The *Cala Galdana* apartment hotel *(closed Dec–March | 75 apartments, 204 rooms | tel. 9 71 15 45 00 | www.hotel calagaldana.com | Expensive)* in the *Hotel*

Country estate, hotel, cheese museum: Hort de Sant Patrici

Paradise white sandy beach with crystal clear water: Cala Galdana

Galdana & Villas d'Aljandar is particularly well suited for family holidays. There is a fitness centre with sauna and sunbathing lawns, the architecture playing a rather secondary role.

If you are looking for unspoilt countryside on Menorca, then near Cala Galdana you should find out what is available under the *agroturisme* (farm holiday) scheme. The *Binisaid* estate *(4 rooms | Ctra. Ferreries–Cala Galdana, km 4.3 | tel. 9 71 15 50 6 3 | www.binisaid.com)*, one of the first "alternative" holiday offers on Menorca, enjoys an enchanting location between the *barrancs*, surrounded by forest and only a few miles from the coast, with stunning beaches nearby and a swimming pool. Cala Galdana is an ideal bathing beach and the charming surroundings, with dozens of undeveloped natural beaches, invite you to undertake voyages of discovery on the water. Motor boats, dinghies and kayaks for the whole family are available at *Sports Nautics (on the beach | tel. 6 76 99 12 44 | May–Oct).*

Several times a week, excursion boats set sail from Cala Galdana out to sea, heading along the south coast. One provider is *Menorca en Barco (mobile tel. 6 05 49 29 93 | www.menorcaenbarco.com).*

CALA MITJANA ● (127 D–E5) (*D5*)

The bay can be reached by a footpath over the cliffs (roughly 1 km/0.6 mile) or by car (1.5 km/1 mile before Cala Galdana to the left). It is worth the walk, because you are rewarded with a long beach with fine white sand followed by a pine forest. The bay is often called "Spain's Caribbean"; for some, it is one of the most beautiful bays in the whole Mediterranean. Follow the path further in an easterly direction and it leads to the lovely, quiet ● *Cala Trebalúger* (approx. an hour's walk, some of it not easy, from Cala Galdana). Unfortunately, access to the bay has been closed by the landowner; however, no one can stop you, not even the owner, from approaching from the sea side (and this also includes a 100 m wide coastal strip).

ES MIGJORN GRAN

(127 F4–5) *(⌂ E–F5)* **Es Migjorn Gran is still relatively new. It was re-founded during the second British occupation in 1769 and since then has barely changed, except for the name of the place which was previously San Cristóbal.**

A few single storey buildings are gathered around a simple church in the small town centre with narrow, quiet streets. In the course of the town's history there has been one outstanding character: Dr Francesc Camps. He found his vocation in the local history of the island and compiled a record of the island's oral history – its songs and legends –, researched ancient customs and traditions, and thereby helped Menorca's younger generation to strengthen those roots needed to withstand an onslaught of over a million visitors from foreign cultures every year.

Numerous caves, sites of prehistoric finds and also the origins of many island legends are to be found in the course of the ravines, which later feed into Cala Trebalúger. These *barrancs* – which, over thousands of years, have carved a channel 50 m/164 ft deep into the limestone – are sheltered from the *tramuntana* winds and have their own mild microclimate so that the "gardens of Menorca" have established themselves here. However, without an expert guide it will be very hard for you to find the access, especially since more and more landowners are denying a right of way. Roughly halfway between Cala Galdana and Cala Sant Tomás you will find two more bays, usually deserted because access is difficult: *Cala Fustam*, a small beach with a backdrop of pine trees and a large cave at the end of the beach on the left and *Cala Escorxada*. Both can only be reached via a difficult path along the coast as the inland paths cross private property and have been blocked.

FOOD & DRINK

CA'NA PILAR

Paquí and José serve traditional, but newly interpreted Menorcan fare in a rustic atmosphere. First-class ingredients, homemade desserts and a romantic terrace. *Ctra. Es Migjorn Gran–Es Mercadal, Av. del Mar 1 (at the entrance to the town)* | *tel. 9 71 37 02 12* | *Moderate–Expensive*

C'AN BERTO

This small pub in the tourist area offers good value for money and very friendly service. Traditional Mediterranean cuisine is served with *montaditos* (canapes) as snacks and meat grilled on a hot stone *(carne a la piedra)* for those with a bigger appetite. Children are welcome! *Urb. Santo Tomás (second row)* | *Moderate*

ES BRUC ● ☼
Chringuito (snack) is the name the Spanish give to their beach restaurants. *Es Bruc* on Sant Adeodat beach combines many of their best qualities: picturesque location overlooking the sea, fresh seafood at reasonable prices. However, in midsummer it can be very congested. *At the end of the Es Migjorn–Sant Tomás main road | Sant Tomás | tel. 9 71 37 04 88 | Moderate*

S'ENGOLIDOR
Here you will get hearty, traditional Menorcan cuisine at reasonable prices. Try the pork ribs done the Menorcan way or the stingray with capers. Great terrace! *Tue–Sun from 7pm | C/ Major 3 | tel. 9 71 37 01 93 | www.sengolidor.com | Budget*

SHOPPING

In Binicudrell – about half a mile southwest from Es Migjorn Gran – the artist

LOW BUDGET

You can save some money by buying the delicious, spicy Menorcan cheese directly from the producer, such as at *Hijo de F. Quintana (Av. Des Camp Verd 47 | Parzelle 47 – Polygono La Trotxa | www.QuesoQuintana.com)* in Alaior or at *Subaida (Mon–Sat 9am–2pm and 5pm–9pm, in Aug also Sun 9am–2pm | Ctra. De Binifabini | www.subaida.com)* in Es Mercadal.

The simple country inn *La Trotxa (C/ La Industri | on the roundabout as you head towards Maó | tel. 9 71 37 87 39)* in Alaior serves a cheap and tasty full daily menu.

Melisa Cabal (Binicudrell de Baix | mobile tel. 6 15 26 58 74 | www.melisacabal.com) runs a small gallery/workshop where she mainly exhibits her own work: very expressive, figurative works, often around the theme "wine". Phone in advance to arrange a visit.

WHERE TO STAY

BINIGAUS VELL ●
This charming country hotel exudes a sense of discreet luxury. It has white facades, splashes of colourful flowers and wooden tools. There is also a stunning outdoor pool and the opportunity to go riding on a horse from their own stables. The 20 comfortable rooms are, however, not exactly cheap. *Camí de Sa Mala Garba, km 0.9 | tel. 9 71 05 40 50 | www.binigausvell.es | Expensive*

INSIDER TIP ▶ S'ENGOLIDOR
If you decide to stay in the town, you can not only enjoy authentic Menorcan cuisine at the restaurant *S'Engolidor* but also get rustic and cosy accommodation – and affordable. Pere Sales and his family will treat you as one of the family. *May–Oct | 5 rooms | C/ Major 3 | tel. 9 71 37 01 93 | www.sengolidor.es | Budget*

INFORMATION
Town hall | Plaça de l'Església | tel. 9 71 37 01 11

WHERE TO GO

COVA DELS COLOMS
(127 F5) (*⍭ E5*)
The locals call the cave, which is only accessible on foot, "the cathedral" because of its considerable size: 24 m/78 ft high, 11 m/36 ft deep and 16 m/52 ft wide. According to the most recent investiga-

tions, it was used in pre-Christian times as a cult site. It is an old superstition of the Menorcans that couples who enter the cave together will separate after a short time; people who meet independently of one another in the cave, however, would be united by the power of fate.

On the way from Es Migjorn Gran down to Sant Tomàs beach there are three archaeological sites. The *Talaiot de Binicudrell* has not been unearthed yet,

PLATJA SANT TOMÀS
(127 F5) *(ṁ E5)*

On the main road from Es Migjorn Gran to the sea you soon come to three beaches separated from one another by narrow rocky outcrops: *Binigaus* to the west, *Sant Adeodat* in the middle and *Sant Tomàs* to the east. The last two are busier, boosted by hotels and a holiday resort at Platja Sant Tomàs. Above the Sant Adeodat beach is a nice ⁇ beach bar. The fantastic sea view is a perfect com-

Mountain biker on the coastal path at Sant Tomás

a but restoration is planned. The prehistoric settlement of *Sant Agustí Vell* is well-known for a large stone building covered with beams which led earlier generations of archaeologists to the conclusion, now outdated, that the *taules* were only central supports for a covering beam construction. The third settlement, *Santa Mónica*, is therefore interesting because here a row of *navetas* (precursors of the *talaiots*) were joined up to create a settlement which was clearly used not as a burial site, but as a dwelling.

plement to a nice snack. The typical qualities of the Sol hotel chain are on offer at the *Sol Elite Menorca (188 rooms | Platja Sant Tomàs | tel. 9 71 37 00 50 | www.melia.com | Expensive)* on the Sant Tomàs beach: comfortable accommodation surrounded by lush gardens. You reach *Binigaus*, the quieter beach, via a footpath along the sea (just under a mile). It is worth the walk for the fine, light grey sand, especially in peak season when the other two beaches are full.

CIUTADELLA/ WESTERN TIP

Everything's all right with the world in Ciutadella. Not perhaps because time has somewhere lost its way from the late Middle Ages to the present, but rather the very opposite: because the peaceful old facades of the houses and palaces conceal an intact, well organised society.

Unemployment only plays a minor role here, many residents are involved in the leather trade, commerce and tourism; the crime rate is low, the quality of life is good. Wool and leather exports and vibrant trade must also have played an important role during the Middle Ages and laid the foundations for the "traditional and stately" Ciutadella which island chroniclers have throughout the years always described with the appropri-

ate measure of respect. Until the 18th century Ciutadella was the island's capital. The capital was moved but the bishop remained and the town (now a National Monument) remains the island's religious capital. A new addition, however, are the large holiday resorts that surround it, such as Cala En Forcat in the west, mainly popular with the British; the luxury holiday homes resort Cala Morell in the north and the constantly expanding resorts of Cala Blanca and Son Xoriguer in the south.

CALA MORELL

(126 C2) (*Ø C2*) The resorts Son Morell and Marina have merged into one holi-

Soft sand and ochre tones, weathered facades, cobbled streets and pastel coloured old town palaces

day resort. Off season the white, uninhabited houses on the slopes of the reddish brown cliffs, eroded by the weather, at Cala Morell bay look rather incongruous.

The architecture of the complex is reminiscent of Ibiza, with some features typical of Menorca, such as the imaginatively installed water outlets which lighten the austere appearance of many homes.

Centuries ago the original inhabitants of Menorca used a small branch of the *cala*

to establish a settlement (around 900 BC) in the soft limestone caves halfway up a cliff. There are just under 20 caves, some with support column and niches, and they are easily accessible from the road. Limestone above, rust-coloured sandstone below – this is where the imaginary line begins which geologists use to separate the much older Tramuntana, the north of the island, from Migjorn, the south of the island. The line runs between Cala Morell and Maó. The small, pebbly beach, however, is not necessarily worth visiting.

CALA MORELL

WHERE TO STAY

BINIATRAM

The rustic country estate is situated about half a mile from the sea, surrounded by unspoilt nature. The property is about 500 cals who had always used the area for swimming and camping – it is now a nature reserve – which led at first to the inhabitants of Ciutadella once more gaining free access, then free access for everyone. (A free parking lot is 500

Ciutadella's port bay cuts deeply into the town like a fjord

years old and has been lovingly restored, with terraces, garden and swimming pool. *12 rooms | Ctra. Cala Morell, km 1 | tel. 9 71 38 31 13 | www.biniatram.com | Moderate*

WHERE TO GO

CALA ALGAIARENS
(126 C2) (*C2*)

Two quiet bays are situated within a huge private estate and they have been making headlines since 1992, because the owner was one of the first to propose charges for access to the beach. This provoked vehement protests by the lo- m/528 yds from the beach). The beach is split in two by a rocky outcrop. The eastern section abuts a small freshwater lagoon, the remains of winter rainfall which runs off via the *La Vall* dyke and flows into the sea here.

CALA SES FONTANELLES
(126 C2) (*C2*)

Not as gentle a slope as the beach at Cala Algaiarens, Cala Ses Fontanelles is popularly used in summer by boat owners who anchor off the cliffs. Road access forks left 1 km/0.6 mile before the road to Cala Algaiarens.

CIUTADELLA

MAP INSIDE BACK COVER
(126 B3) *(⊞ B3–4)* **Although with 29,000 inhabitants a little bigger than Maó, daily life in ★ Ciutadella is lived at a more leisurely pace than in the vibrant rival town. People seem to have more time here than in the hustle and bustle of Maó.**

Everyday life runs at a more even tempo, perhaps also a little more humane. Here the barber, when he runs out of customers in the afternoon, will warm himself a bit in the setting sun on a folding chair outside his shop. Here a stranger is often greeted with a nod of the head and the older generation here still have plenty to say, usually in a haze of thick cigar smoke and in an animated *tertulia* (discussion group) in the *Cercle Artistic* or in the shadow of the obelisk which stands like an admonishing finger over Plaça d'es Born as a reminder of the destruction of the town by a Turkish naval unit. More than 500 years have passed since that bloody attack: more than 3000 people were enslaved, the town plundered and razed to the ground so that people were forced to start again from scratch. In the 16th and 17th century the town flourished once again. Churches and monasteries were established, the centre was enclosed by town walls and it was at first home to the island diocese before finally becaming the Menorcan capital – until the occupation of the island by the British in 1722. It was only after the end of the Franco dictatorship that the island council allowed a referendum as to decide which of the two major towns should become the administrative centre of Menorca. Ciutadella was defeated by only a few votes.

SIGHTSEEING

BAIXADA CAPLLONCH (U D4) *(⊞ d4)*
The *Ca'n Squella* palace and the bishop's palace *Palau Episcopal* (both 17th century) are situated on the edge of Carrer Sant Sebastia and Carrer del Bisbé. In the quiet streets the aroma of fresh bread still wafts from many a bakery in the morning. Further to the west the steps come into view leading down to the sea. The steps down to the docks are lined with souvenir stalls, boutiques and shops. To the right round the corner you come to popular *Café Balear* (see Food & Drink).

MARCO POLO HIGHLIGHTS

★ **Ciutadella**
Without doubt the most beautiful spot on the island: old and distinguished, with life lived at a leisurely pace. It is also an ideal base for exciting voyages of discovery → p. 77

★ **Boat tours**
Take a trip around Cap d'Artrutx to the paradise bays in the island's south → p. 83

★ **Cala Macarella**
White sand and turquoise water bordered by grey limestone → p. 87

★ **Cala en Turqueta**
A stunning bay with a gently sloping sandy beach, shady pine trees and coastal cliffs → p. 88

★ **Nau des Tudons**
The oldest known building in Europe → p. 88

Exhibits in the Museu Municipal in the Bastió de sa Font

BASTIÓ DE SA FONT
(U F3–4) (*f3–4*)

The original fortress from the 14th century was destroyed in 1558 by the Turks and not rebuilt until the end of the 17th century. It houses the ● *Museu Municipal* which documents Menorca's chequered history – its prehistory and the Muslim occupation – with with multimedia exhibits, finds, historic documents, writings and the like. *Tue–Sat 10am–2pm, May–Sept also 6pm–9pm | admission 2.46 euros (Wed free) / Plaça de Sa Font 15*

CAPELLA DEL SANT CRIST
(U E5) (*e5*)

On the corner of Carrer del Seminari and Carrer del Sant Crist stands the Capella del Sant Crist (construction started in 1667). The small domed structure was expensive for the sheep shearers who, during the Middle Ages, provided the port of Ciutadella with wool, one of its most important exports.

CASTELL DE SANT NICOLAU (0) (*0*)

The octagonal watch tower from the 17th century was once part of the town defences. *Tue–Sat 10am–1pm | Passeig Marítim*

CATEDRAL ●
(U D4–5) (*d4–5*)

The Carrer Major d'es Born leads to the cathedral on Plaça de la Catedral. It owes its massive, angular appearance not least to a reinforcement of the structure after part of the dome collapsed in 1628. In 1795 a papal edict elevated the new building to the status of Cathedral of Menorca, provoking considerable criticism from Maó. The current bell tower dates back to the minaret of a mosque which dominated the square until the 13th century *(Mon–Sat 10am–4pm)*. Countless anecdotes and legends surround the church. It is said that, when the new building was constructed, the window frames had to be sealed because hundreds of birds got into the church whilst prayers were being said. In the course of history the cathedral also became a place of refuge for many people who had fallen into disfavour with the island governors of the time. Sacral treasures are on exhibition in the vestry and chapter room, including a silver rosary madonna. *Admission 3 euros, combined with the Església del Socors 5 euros*

ESGLÉSIA DEL ROSER (U D5) (*m d5*)

Carrer del Roser branches off in a southerly direction from opposite the *Porta de la Llum* (light gate), the entrance to the cathedral on the right. After fifty paces you come to the narrow facade of the *Església del Roser* which was built from 1664 on the foundations of an older church and today is only opened for exhibitions.

ESGLÉSIA DEL SOCORS/MUSEU DIOCESÀ (U D5) (*m d5*)

Founded in 1648, this Augustinian monastery today houses the *Museu Diocesà*, a museum exhibiting archaeological finds, stuffed animals and paintings by local artists. The cloister and church alone are worth the visit. **INSIDER TIP** Classical concerts are held here as part of the summer festival *Festival Musica d'Estiu*.

MARINA (U C3–4) (*m c3–4*)

In Ciutadella's port there is a striking difference between the right bank, used by commercial and passenger traffic, and the left bank. On the left, by the marina, there is a row of exclusive restaurants, serving well-heeled guests fresh fish.

MERCAT (MARKET HALL) ●
(U E6) (*m e6*)

The sun only penetrates the small, quiet alleys around the market hall at around midday. But nonetheless at the *Mercat*, the market, a Mediterranean ambience

characterises the scene. In the white and dark grey tiled building each guild takes up one side, the butchers looking across to the other side of Carrer de la Palma with a series of vegetable stalls and traditional market bars.

PALAU OLIVAR (U D4) (*m d4*)

Opposite the cathedral the palace of Señor Luis de Oliver can be visited: noble halls with frescos; there's a curious frieze with all the animals on Noah's ark. Level with the palace was where formerly the *judería*, the Jewish quarter began (Carrer Palau, Carrer Sant Jeroni and Carrer Sant Francesc), with a row of simple town houses. *Mon–Sat 10am–2pm | admission 3 euros | Plaça de la Catedral 8*

PALAU SALORT (U C–D4) (*m c–d4*)

In the splendid palace at the top of the main road in the old town, you can wander through the majestic rooms belonging to the noble family, Torre-Saura. *Mon–Sat 10am–2pm | admission 2.50 euros | Major d'es Born*

PLAÇA D'ES BORN (U C4) (*m c4*)

The obelisk on Plaça d'es Born is a reminder of the *Any de sa Desgracia* (year of disaster). It casts its shadow every morning on the *town hall (Ajuntament)* which was once an Arabian fortress, then the castle of King Alfonso III – who liberated the town and island from the Moors – and later the residence of several island governors. The present building dates from the 19th century. Every year on 9 July a commemoration takes place on the square recalling the event when 15,000 "infidels" laid siege to the town in 1558. It also celebrates the heroes of Ciutadella who, for seven days, bravely defied the superior forces before the town fell and was almost totally de-

The red-brown sandstone is a hallmark of Ciutadella: city palace at the Plaça d'es Born

stroyed. Behind the town hall an ❋ **INSIDER TIP** *observation deck (Mirador)* on the town walls, the *Bastió des Governador (daily 9am–1pm),* grants a magnificent panoramic views.

SES VOLTES (U E5) (Ⓜ *e5*)

Ses Voltes is the name of the arcades which line *Carrer Josep M. Ouadrado* on both sides. Retail trade and small businesses thrive in the shade of the arches, each one individual and unlike any of the others. The bars on the adjoining *Plaça Nova* are usually very full, with mainly newcomers to the town enjoying a rest and a coke or lemonade. Keep going straight on and you come to *Plaça Alfons III* or *Plaça de Ses Palmeres,* as the townspeople call it, and from there to *Camí de Maó* which spans the island up to the east coast. To the west is *C/ Sant Antoni,* then *C/ Sant Josep.* Here you will find restaurants and cafés mostly fre-

quented by locals. To the right at the end of *C/ Santa Clara* you come to the palace of the Baron of Lluriach *(Castell Lluriach),* the first nobleman of Menorca, appointed by Charles II after the battle with the Arab occupiers on Spain's south coast.

TOWN PALACES
(U C–D 4–5) (Ⓜ *c–d 4–5*)

In the afternoon the obelisk casts its shadow on the facades of the east side of *Plaça d'es Born.* There are a number of cafés, souvenir shops and restaurants on the lower floors of the palaces *Palau Torresaura, Palau Vivó* and *Palau Salort,* all built in *marés,* that breathable, golden brown sandstone which was a form of building air conditioning in the past. Guided tours of the town – including the palaces – are offered by *Talaia Cultura (mobile tel. 6 60 42 52 54 | www.talaia cultura.com).*

To the north of the square is the *Cercle Artístic* – founded in 1881 and renovated at the beginning of the 1990s – and the *Teatre Municipal d'es Born*, the town theatre. In the "art circle" it is not usually art that is the topic of the day, but rather the current political issues, people sometimes being quite voluble. In the adjacent theatre, films are shown, plays performed and there is the occasional musical event. Opposite you will find the main post office, several bars and the *Sant Francesc* monastery chapel, built in 1627 on the site of an older church destroyed by pirates.

FOOD & DRINK

CAFÉ BALEAR (U D4–5) (🗺 d4–5)
Popular tapas and seafood stop for tourists and locals alike. The small restaurant has become an island institution with its good lunch menu and delicious seafood

specialities. *Daily in the main season | Pla de Sant Joan 12 | tel. 9 71 38 00 05 | www. cafebalear.com | Moderate–Expesive*

LA CAYENA (U E6) (🗺 e6)
Housed in a building with a small patio in the old town centre, they serve delicious fusion cuisine with an Asian influence. Exposed sandstone walls display modern art. This is the right place for a romantic evening out as it is off the beaten track. Head next door to the **INSIDER TIP** *Café Viajero*, or the "travel café", where you can enjoy home-made sweet pastries, filled bagels and pasties while browsing through travel literature or visiting one of their travel film evenings. *Closed Sun | C/ Alaior 40 | tel. 9 71 48 22 12 | lacayena. blogspot.com.es | Moderate*

DES PORT (U C4) (🗺 c4)
From this harbour restaurant in blue and white decor, you can gaze out over the harbour's fisher boats while enjoying exciting Menorcan cuisine prepared by the chef Tolo. Why not try his salad with local cheese and tomato chutney followed by sea bream with rocket or tender lamb filet on a bed of sliced potatoes? The large rock cave provides perfect shelter in bad weather. *Daily | C/ de Marina 23 | tel. 9 71 48 17 35 | Moderate*

ES LLOC (0) (🗺 0)
The restaurant is in the hotel *Sant Ignaci*, housed in a beautifully restored 18th century manor house. Good Mediterranean specialities. *Ctra. Cala Morell | to the left behind the industrial area | tel. 9 71 38 55 75 | Expensive*

LA GUITARRA (U D5) (🗺 d5)
In their lively cellar bar or on the terrace, Gabriel and Izaskun serve tasty and traditional Balearic cuisine such as *frito marinero* (fried seafood), *baca-*

lao (cod with a honey and aioli crust) and tumbet (stewed vegetables). The **INSIDER TIP** homemade mascarpone ice cream is the icing on the cake. *Closed*

INSIDER TIP Wednesday evenings (from 8pm) for a token price! Friday is wine-tasting evening with a selection of local Menorcan wines to try. *C/ Ses Voltes 16–*

A landmark in Ciutadella's old town – the restaurant Ses Voltes

Sun | C/ Dolores 1 | tel. 9 71 38 13 55 | Moderate

SES VOLTES (U D5) (*ω d5*)

This establishment welcomes visitors from early morning to late in the night. A filling sandwich for breakfast, a snack for lunch and a fine-dining meal in the evening – this restaurant celebrates the best of what Menorcan cuisine has to offer. Housed in a three-storey old town house at the heart of Ciutadella, the restaurant serves tapas on the ground floor and à la carte menu on the first floor and on its rooftop terrace. Pintxos & cañas (diverse snacks on a stick and beer) are available on

22 | tel. 9 71 38 14 98 | www.recibaria. com | Budget–Expensive

SHOPPING

EL PALADAR (0) (*ω 0*)

Exquisite Menorcan products including sausage, ham, cheeses, Menorca honey, wine and herbal liqueurs. You can also enjoy a light bite here. *Ca/ de la Creu 1 and C/ Maó 10 | www.elpaladar.es*

INSIDER TIP GRANEL

(U D5) (*ω d5*)

Ciutadella's most appealing delicatessen selling a wide assortment of island speci-alities such as cheeses, smoked sausages, sweet pastries, jams, honey, liquors, wine, gin, dried herbs etc. Feel free to try everything before you buy. *Ses Voltes 8 | www.granel.cat*

JAP – ARTÍCULOS TÍPICOS
(U D4) *(m d4)*

Typical Menorcan souvenirs, especially leather goods, in a little shop near the port. *Baixada Capllonch 12*

PACHAMAMA
(U C4–5) *(m c4–5)*

Affordable accessories: handmade costume jewellery and paste gems. *Plaça d'es Born 27–28*

PATRICIA
(U D5) *(m d5)*

You can buy all sorts of beautiful leather goods, with the emphasis on clothes, belts, bags and shoes, not only here in the shop *(Josep Cavaller i Piris 5)*, but also (sometimes more cheaply) from the factory on the main road south *(Ctra. de Santandría)*. *www.patricia.es*

SPORTS & ACTIVITIES

BOAT TOURS ★

Boat trips with *Rutas Marítimas de la Cruz (rutasmaritimasdelacruz.com)* or *Menorca Blava (www.menorcablava. com)* take you to remote beaches and bathing bays which often are otherwise not accessible. The glass bottom boats sail up the west and part of the south coast. Day trips will take you to the southwest via *Cala en Bosc* and *Cala de Son Saura* to *Cala Galdana*, in summer with a break for a swim. The boats set sail in summer *daily at 10am*, returning about *5pm*. They depart from the port in Ciutadella *(Pantalón 1)*. You can buy tickets in advance in several shops at the port. Information: *tel. 9 71 35 07 78*

SAILING (0) *(m 0)*

You can hire boats of all kinds, from dinghy to yacht, at *Sports Massanet | Motonáutica | C | Marina 78 | tel. 9 71 48 42 81 | www.menorcaboats.com.*

DIVING (0) *(m 0)*

The western tip of Menorca provides a rich and varied marine life and a wide range of diving centres. One well-established *PADI diving centre (Cala en Busqutes 10 | Edificio Las Terrazas | tel. 6 96 90 31 60 | www.scubaplus.org)* is right next to the exit to Ciutadella port.

LOW BUDGET

When the connection is available, you can use the free WiFi in the town library. *Biblioteca Pública de Ciutadella (Casa de Cultura | Hospital de Santa Magdalena 1 | in summer Mon–Fri 9.30am–1.30pm and 6pm–8pm, in winter Mon–Fri 10am–1pm and 4pm–8pm)*

If you want to save fuel and go by bike, you can hire one at *Velos Joan* in Ciutadella *(C/ Sant Isidre 32–34 | tel. 9 71 38 15 76 | www.velosjoan. com)* or Maó *(Av. Francesc Femenias 58 | tel. 9 71 36 99 79)*. They have very reasonable weekly rates.

A unique offer: buy a fish on the market in Ciutadella and let the chef in *Ulises (closed Sun | Plaça Mercat | tel. 9 71 38 00 31)* fry it for you for a modest price (2–4 euros depending on the size) where you can then eat it. The breakfast and daily specials are also reasonable and there is sheltered seating under the market's arcades.

It offers training, equipment hire and diving.

TENNIS (0) (*Ⓜ 0*)

Public tennis court with floodlights: *Club de Tenis Ciutadella (Torre del Ram | tel. 9 71 38 84 56 | www.clubtenisciutadella. com)*

ENTERTAINMENT

Ciutadella is the hotspot on Menorca's nightlife scene and the city especially comes to life on Saturdays. Flyers are handed out during the week advertising free entry (usually for women only) or a free drink. The locals like to start a night out on Menorca with a hearty *pa amb oli* (bread with tomatoes, garlic and olive oil), e.g. in the **INSIDER TIP** *Ses Persianas (Plaça d'Artrutx 2)* or in the *Sa Barreta (C/ José María Quadrado 22)*. Then they look in at the beautifully renovated and very popular *Imperi (Plaça d'es Born 7)* – to see and be seen. Here. you eat a hearty *llonguet*, a filled Menorca roll.

The late night bars in the port area of *Es Pla de Sant Joan* are very fashionable. Where just a few years ago fishermen hauled their *llauts* ashore to repaint them in the shade of the boat houses, today there are pale flashing neon lights. This is where some of the best dance clubs are to be found: *Jazzbah (Es Pla 3)*, now a landmark on the city's club scene, still attracts large crowds. Top forty hits are played downstairs while upstairs on the rooftop terrace you can chill out with a cocktail or glass of beer. What was once the legendary Esfera club is now *Kopas (Sat 11.30pm–5.30am | www.kopasclub. com)* and, like *Jazzbah*, frequently organises live events. Guests can dance and chill out on the various floors while the rooftop terrace offers panoramic views over the entertainment district of Es Pla.

If you're looking for something more low-key, and a cool drink accompanied by the sea's breeze sounds appealing, head for one of the many street bars – their prices are far less expensive than those in the clubs (4–6 euros). *Ones (www.pubmusicalones.com)* is an uncomplicated option while the new *Shisha Club* smoking lounge offers guests (nicotine-free) hookahs with a variety of flavours. Another cheek-by-jowl location in the evening is Ses Voltes and the streets around. Here you can find quieter bars and pubs such as *La Moncloa* at the Plaça Nova and *Can Colás* at Carrer Alaior. One of the largest discos in the west of the island is *Anchors (in the Son Oleo district),* a stylish club with spectacular lighting effects, a mixture of music and guests as well as live acts in summer. If you're still not ready to turn in for the night, follow the groups of fishermen starting their day in the **INSIDER TIP** *Triton (down at the jetty)*.

WHERE TO STAY

CIUTADELLA (U E6) (*Ⓜ e6*)

A basic Hostal Residencia right in the centre, many rooms with en-suite bathroom and the in-house restaurant serves good regional cuisine. *17 rooms | C/ Sant Eloi 10 | tel. 9 71 38 34 62 | all year | Budget–Moderate*

HOSTAL OASIS (U E6) (*Ⓜ e6*)

This Bed & Breakfast in the old town was named after the romantic garden in its courtyard. It is the most affordable accommodation far and wide with friendly, practical rooms (double room with shared bathroom 29 euros, and 35 euros with a private bathroom). Señor Nuno makes your stay truly pleasurable. *12 rooms | C/ Sant Isidre 33 | mobile tel. 6 30 01 80 08 | www.hostaloasismenorca.es | Budget*

INSIDER TIP PORT
CIUTADELLA(O) *(Ⱥ O)*

This well-maintained four-star hotel in a prime location has its own bathing access to the sea (no beach!) and is located on the outskirts of Ciutadella. It has an indoor and outdoor pool, jacuzzi, steam bath, sauna and a small beauty centre with upmarket treatments. Many rooms have balconies and a view over the bay; relaxed atmosphere thanks to the friendly, helpful staff. Free WiFi. *94 rooms and suites | Passeig Marítim 36 | tel. 9 71 48 25 20 | www.sethotels.com/es/port-ciutadella-hotel.html | Expensive*

RIFUGIO AZUL (U D5) *(Ⱥ d5)*

Located in the old part of the city, the "Blue Refuge" has a friendly and enthusiastic owner, Mattia, who makes you feel immediately at home. Modern, welcoming rooms (free WiFi, air conditioning) and a suite with terrace and Jacuzzi. Excellent breakfast with home-made cake. *4 rooms | C/ ses Andrones 33 | mobile tel. 6 34 22 68 23 | www.rifugioazul.com | Moderate*

971 (U D5) *(Ⱥ d5)*

In a top central old town location nestled between the harbour and cathedral, this small Italian-run hotel was inspired by Italo Calvino's novel "Invisible Cities": contemporarily furnished rooms in a historic palace with a touch of eccentricity. *6 rooms, 1 apartment | C/ Sant Sebastiá 10 | mobile tel. 6 48 19 69 73 | www.971menorca.com | Moderate*

INFORMATION

OFICINA DE INFORMACIÓN TURÍSTICA (U C4) *(Ⱥ c4)*
Plaça d'es Born 15 | Tel. 9 71 48 41 55 | www.menorca.es

There is always plenty going on in Ciutadella

BUSES

The intercity bus station *(TMSA bus company | tel. 9 71 36 04 75 | www.tmsa.es)* is located to the south of the old town at the Plaça de la Pau. The terminal for inner-city buses travelling to destinations in and around Ciutadella is in the old town at the Plaça de s'Explanada/ Plaça des Pins *(Torres bus company | tel. 9 02 07 50 66 | www.bustorresmenorca.com)*. Be warned: the frequency of buses depends on the time of year!

WHERE TO GO

CALA BLANCA (126 B4) *(Ⱥ B4)*
The name refers both to the holiday resort (approx. 4 km/2.5 miles south of Ciutadella) — with no particular features to distinguish it from comparable resorts on the island — and to the bay situated

on the southern edge of the resort. It owes its name (white bay) to the brilliant white sand framed by the green backdrop of a pine forest of trees. To the left and right of the beach are the coastal cliffs covered with restaurants and bars, which are better for their outstanding location rather than for remarkable food. The ☀ view of a romantic sunset is pretty much guaranteed here on most evenings. For children there is a water slide in the resort and *Cova de Parella*, well-known for its stalactites and stalagmites and a subterranean lake, is situated not far from the bay.

On the main road to Cap d'Artrutx, just before Cala Blanca, is *Es Caliu (tel. 9 71 38 01 65 | Budget–Moderate)*, a mix of beach club and drive-in, with swimming pool, barbecue specialities in the evening and still reasonable prices. Although it gets overcrowded in summer, the large restaurant *Cala Blanca (daily | Av. Llevant 1 | tel. 9 71 38 27 01 | www.restaurantecalablanca.com | Moderate)* is famous for its speciality Paella and its seaside setting offers a nice sea breeze and the perfect place to watch the evening sunset. Another waterfront restaurant, *Miramar (daily | Av. Cala Blanca | tel. 9 71 38 62 62 | Moderate),* serves fish and meat grilled on a hot stone.

CALA EN BOSC (126 B5) (*ω B5*)

From the Cap d'Artrutx resort you come to Cala en Bosc, the next holiday paradise. Here too the architecture of the resort is no more than average, based more on functionality than aesthetics, but the beach on the edge of the resort with fine white sand and usually clean sea water speaks for itself. Informal *chiringuitos* (beach bars) cater to every taste. The area between Cap d'Artrutx and Son Xoriguer is where the *minitren* runs, a small tourist train on rubber wheels. Boats and yachts can be hired from *P&F (tel. 6 10 26 12 91).* The established water sports school *Surf & Sail (on Son Xoriguer beach | mobile tel. 6 29 74 99 44)* offers windsurfing and sailing courses in summer.

A quieter side cove of the Cala Macarella is the Cala Macarelleta

CALA D'ES DEGOLLADOR
(126 B3) (*m B4*)

The spit of land just south of the entrance to the port of Ciutadella owes its gruesome name (cut-throat bay) not, as you might have thought, to the beach sellers offering overpriced drinks, but to a pirate attack a long time ago. The small beach is mainly used for bathing by the inhabitants of Ciutadella.

CALA EN FORCAT
(126 A–B3) (*m A3–4*)

A holiday village on the coastal cliff to the west of Ciutadella. The resorts of *Cala en Blanes, Cala en Forcat* and *Cala en Brut* have become so enmeshed with the resort of *Los Delfines* that it is hard to see where one resort ends and another begins. The coastline is occupied by a number of villas with stunning sea views. Each of the bays has at least one small beach. The largest is the one at *Cala en Blanes,* around 50 m/165 ft wide. However, you will look here in vain for wide, empty beaches – at least in summer. On the western edge of *Cala en Forcat* there are some striking sea water geysers. These *bufadors* are, however, not the result of volcanic activities, but of a system of caves and ducts reacting to the water pressure. The *Globales Club Almirante Farragut (May–Oct | 472 rooms | tel. 9 71 38 80 00 | www.hotelalmirantefa rragut.com | Moderate–Expensive)* is a tasteful three-star hotel.

CALA MACARELLA ★
(127 D5) (*m D5*)

This is Menorca's version of paradise: clear turquoise water, bordered by a ring of grey limestone, in the background the strip of sand and a small wetland where turtles once lived. The access road is long and stony and there is a 5 euros charge of per car, ● which you can save if you park before the entrance and then walk. Sometimes, unfortunately, the beach is not as clean as it should be; quite often there is flotsam on the shore and picnic waste in the wood. At the moment, only a bar hidden in the pines caters for beachgoer's needs with simple (and overpriced) dishes. In the cliffs along the shore there are some prehistoric caves. There is a footpath branching off to the west to *Cala Macarelleta,* a nudist retreat.

CALA PAREJALS
(126 B5) (*m B5*)

This is a place especially popular with weekend anglers from Ciutadella who come here to fish, and divers who like to explore the rich and varied underwater world. Access is via a coastal path from *Platja de Son Xoriguer.*

CALA SANTANDRIA
(126 B4) (*m B4*)

This is a pioneering centre of the tourist industry which is still relatively new on Menorca. Lots of bare rock, lots of buildings, hotels, bars, villas, restaurants – and not much greenery. The beach is white and rather gritty. The entrance to the bay is guarded by an old 18th century British defence tower. What is especially interesting is the ● INSIDER TIP cave which Nicolau Cabrisas, the sculptor and local celebrity, used as a home and workshop. Over the years the freelance artist covered his home and workshop with masks, grotesque faces and figurines. His life's work can still be visited, even after the master's death, as his wife provides tours if and when she has the time.

The artist has also designed the adjacent restaurant INSIDER TIP *Sa Nacra (Cala Santandria, on the northern shore of the bay | tel. 9 71 38 62 06 | Budget– Moderate)* built directly into the cliff, with stunning romantic sunsets, candle-lit dinners, great tapas and affordable wines. At lunchtime there is really delicious paella. But beware: in high season you will not get in without a reservation. The *Bahía (15 rooms | C/ dels Suissos 3 | tel. 9 71 38 26 44 | www.bahia-poseidon.de/joomla_eng | Moderate)* is a small, friendly family hotel with the additional advantage that it is right next to the beach and the Poseidon diving school. At *Pedro's (C/ d'en Clates)* nightclub from May to September there is a firework display every night with laser shows and karaoke, flamenco and foam parties.

CALA DE SON SAURA
(126 C5) (*∅ C5*)

This bay is ideal for a day on the beach. It is sheltered from the wind and has two beaches, separated by a small spit of land, with fine white sand and pine trees. But beware: there are sometimes strong currents around the bay. To get here from Ciutadella you take Camí de Sant Joan de Missa at the white church of the same name and turn off right at *Son Vivó* going past the old square *Torre Saura Vell* tower. Road access to the beach is subject to a charge. The people of Ciutadella have developed a fondness for Son Saura. If the long beach is already full, a trek eastwards is worthwhile. After crossing the rocky outcrop of *Punta d'es Governador* (approx. 500 m) you come to the next, considerably smaller bay, *Cala d'es Talaier*. The sand is ochre coloured and there is also a pine forest that provides shelter from the sun.

CALA EN TURQUETA ★
(126 C5) (*∅ C5*)

Along with Cala Macarella this has become the epitome of the stunning bays in the south of Menorca. Access from Ciutadella is via Camí de Sant Joan de Missa, bearing left at the fork at Son Vivó. After around 5 km/3 miles the road forks: left takes you to Cala Macarella, right to Cala En Turqueta. The car parks are often full at weekends.

NAU DES TUDONS ★
(126 C3) (*∅ C3*)

The island's most well-known prehistoric grave and probably the oldest known building in Europe. The mighty sandstone blocks were assembled approx. 3400 years ago. In the course of the excavation the team found pieces of jewellery and the remains of human bones, suggesting that this was a plundered burial chamber.

The interior of the *nau* (Spanish *naveta*) is divided in two floors. There is a legend attached to the structure: two giants are said to have argued about a lady. As proof of their love, one was to build a two-storey tower, the other to dig a well until he found water, the first to finish won the lady's hand. The water flowed first and that so enraged the other giant that he broke a huge stone from his tower (the current entrance hole) and threw it at the giant who had dug the well, killing him. The villain then drowned himself in the well and the lady died of a broken heart. The well is still known by the name *Pou de Sa Barrina* today. *Ctra. Me-1 between Ciutadella and Ferreries, km 40*

PUNTA NATI ● �઀
(126 B2) (*∅ B2*)

Some sheep come here looking for the herbs that sprout between the craggy rocks. In spring the inhabitants of Ciutadella also put up with the bumpy access road to Punta Nati *(Av. Francesc B. Moll)* when there are capers growing in the shade of the walls at the cape. The cape has been crowned by a lighthouse since 1913, from which at night you have a fantastic view of the stars in the sky and, during the day, of the sea, the rugged coastline and two bays in the east, *Cala es Pous* and *Cala es Morts* (bay of the dead). This name is based on the incident which occurred in the winter of 1910

Here you will find cisterns, the foundations of living areas, five stone towers *(talaiots)* and the central shrine, the *taula*. The age of the site is still unknown; all that is certain is that it was inhabited until the end of the Roman occupation.

Take the plunge from a yacht into the Cala en Turqueta

when a French passenger ship steered into the cliffs and sank. Of the 150 people on board, only one young Frenchman survived the accident. Today a cross still marks the incident.

SON CATLAR
(126 C4) (*ω C4*)
Before you reach the tower *Torre Saura Vell* on the way from Ciutadella to here, you will see to your left the largest prehistoric settlement area in the whole Balearics, spread over 15 acres and surrounded in part by a partly ruined wall.

Admission 3 euros | access via the path to the Platja de Son Saura

TORRE LLAFUDA
(127 D3) (*ω C3–4*)
This large prehistoric settlement – which is today losing the fight to a steadily encroaching grove of holly oaks – has a magical, almost eerie feel to it. There are rooms, chambers, artificial caves, cisterns, a stone tower and a INSIDER TIP *taula*, all in the shade of the trees. *Access via the main Ciutadella–Maó road, km, then right after about 250 m/273 yds*

DISCOVERY TOURS

1 MENORCA AT A GLANCE

START: ① Binibèquer Vell
END: ⑬ Cap d'Artrutx

Distance:
➡ 140 km/87 miles

2 days
Driving time
(without stops)
3 ½ hours

COSTS: Starting from 30 euros a day for car hire, approx. 18 euros for petrol, 20 euros for food per person, overnight accommodation in Es Migjorn Gran (S'Engolidor) approx. 50 euros for a double room

WHAT TO PACK: Swimwear, sun protection and picnic, if you'd like

IMPORTANT TIPS: If you can, start your tour on a Wednesday to coincide with the market held in ⑦ Alaior.

Every corner of the earth has its own special charm. If you want to explore all the many different facets of this region, head off the beaten track or get tips for the best stops, breathtaking views, hand-picked restaurants or the best local activities, then these customised discovery tours are just the right thing. Choose the best route for the day and follow in the footsteps of the MARCO POLO authors – well-prepared to navigate your way to all the many highlights that await you along the tour.

Menorca's network of roads resembles a fish's skeleton: the island is bisected by the main vertebral spine, the Me-1 motorway, running between Maó in the east and Ciutadella in the west, with smaller roads branching off to the coast in the north and south. This tour takes you from east to west and then from north to south, to the island's former and present day capital, to lively harbours and dormant villages, to paradise bays and rugged capes – explore the island's diversity on this unique tour.

The starting point is ❶ **Binibèquer Vell** → p. 50 with a Mediterranean breakfast of croissants and a steaming cup of *café amb llet* (milky coffee) at the **Club Náutico**. The pic-

DAY 1

❶ Binibèquer Vell

Menorca

Cap de Cavalleria

5 km
3.1 mi

Cova Rolida

Cala Morell   Binimel·la   Fornells

Ciutadella   Es   Port d'Addaia
Me1   Mercadal
Ferreries
Naveta d'Es
Tudons   Cala
Cala   Sta. Galdana
Blanca
Es Migjorn
Gran S. Cristóbal
Es-Grau

Alaior

Cap
d'Artrutx   Tamarinda   Cala
Turqueta   Sant Tomàs

Son Bou   de Baix d'en Gaumes

Talati
de d'Alt

Cala Mesquida

Torre

**Maó
(Mahón)**

Sant Lluís

Cala En Porter   Sant
Cova d'En Xoroi   Climent

S' Algar

Mar Mediterrània   Binibequer Vell

Punta Prima

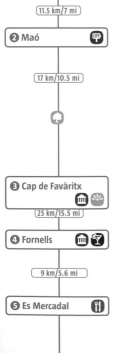

11.5 km/7 mi

2 Maó

17 km/10.5 mi

3 Cap de Favàritx

25 km/15.5 mi

4 Fornells

9 km/5.6 mi

5 Es Mercadal

ture-perfect resort in the south-east of Menorca is a rep-
lica of a traditional pirate's cove. **From here it is about a
20 minute drive to ② Maó → p. 36** where you can take
in a first glance of the city by walking from the Plaça de
s'Esplanada (with car park and tourist information) to the
old town and from there down to the harbour. **To leave the
city, head along the quieter Ronda de Sant Joan, which
from the left joins the Me-7 main road to Fornells.** From
here the landscape becomes gentler, greener and more
tranquil and you will soon be driving through the island's
nature reserves in the north east.

**About halfway along the route, a country road (Cf-1) on
your right leads to the lighthouse at ③ Cap de Favàritx
→ p. 57,** which stands on weathered cliffs above the
sea, representing the remote, rugged face of the island.
Back on the Me-7 carry on to the small coastal resort of
④ Fornells → p. 52. Perched on the banks of the great
salt water lagoon, with fishing boats reflected in the
tranquil waters, you can enjoy a cool drink at the **Bar La
Palma** before leaving. Don't be tempted to a snack because your lunch time destination is not far away. **Head
south on the Me-15 to ⑤ Es Mercadal → p. 58,** popular for its restaurants serving tasty, local food. After your
meal the tour continues south, leaving the steppe land-

scape of the north coast behind to embrace pine groves which then in turn give way to the lush green pastures in the centre of the island. **On the eastern outskirts of this small town, a narrow tarmac road leads up to the barren ⑥ Monte Toro → p. 59.** After a few hairpin bends you reach a height of 357 m/1171 ft. From the "roof of Menorca" you can enjoy a fantastic panoramic view. Although you've just finished lunch in Es Mercadal, try to squeeze in a pastry and coffee in the delightful **monastery restaurant Sa Posada del Toro. En route to Maó a detour then leads you to ⑦ Alaior → p. 63,** a traditional resort famous for its arts and crafts and cheese dairies. The village market held on Wednesdays (from 7pm onwards) is a good opportunity to check out local crafts and buy some of the delicious specialities. **Back on the road to Ciutadella, the Me-16 turns off to the right after about 3 km/2.2 miles to the sleepy resort of ⑧ Es Migjorn Gran → p. 71.** After a splendid meal at the delightful guesthouse **S'Engolidor** you can also spend the night here.

Enjoy a full breakfast **before continuing along the Me 20 and later along hairpin bends cut into the reddish brown rock cliffs to Cala Galdana.** Schedule a break at **⑨ Ferreries → p. 67** to take in the charm of the old part of town perched on the hill. **Then about 300 m/985 ft after leaving the resort, turn left onto the smaller Me-22 road.** After just under 5 km/3 miles you will be treated to a wonderful view of white sandy beaches and turquoise sea of **⑩ Cala Galdana → p. 69.** Take a refreshing plunge into the waves before enjoying lunch at the restaurant **El Mirador.**

Back on the Me-1, drive westwards and just before you reach the outskirts of Ciutadella, follow the road signposted on your left to one of the oldest buildings in Europe. Do not miss out on a visit to the **⑪ Nau des Tudons → p. 88:** wander between the gigantic stones which appear to have been erected by giants. Now drive on to **⑫ Ciutadella → p. 77,** the largest city in the west of the island and regarded by some as Spain's most beautiful. **Park near the Plaça de ses Palmeras (Alfonso III)** where you can start to explore this vibrant town by strolling along the Carrer de Maó and Carrer de Josep Maria Quadrado and then down to Plaça d'es Born.

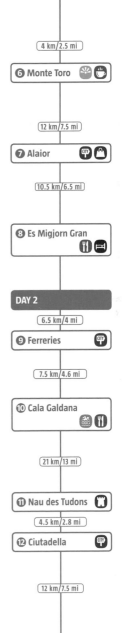

4 km/2.5 mi

⑥ Monte Toro

12 km/7.5 mi

⑦ Alaior

10.5 km/6.5 mi

⑧ Es Migjorn Gran

DAY 2

6.5 km/4 mi

⑨ Ferreries

7.5 km/4.6 mi

⑩ Cala Galdana

21 km/13 mi

⑪ Nau des Tudons

4.5 km/2.8 mi

⑫ Ciutadella

12 km/7.5 mi

Then drive south along the Me-24 until you reach the spectacularly wild and rugged ⑬ **Cap d'Artrutx** ewith its lighthouse. How about a dip in the sea at the beautiful tiny beach of **Cala en Bosc**, before ending your evening in style at the lighthouse? Many visitors gather here in summer to enjoy a bottle of wine while watching the INSIDER TIP sunset The rays of light transform the sea into vivid colours of yellow to saffron red. When the sun finally disappears, the spectacle is accompanied with a rapturous round of applause...

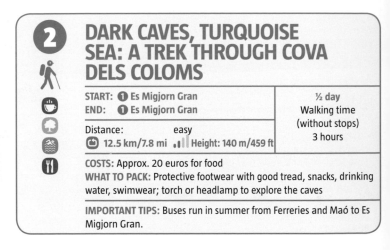

2 DARK CAVES, TURQUOISE SEA: A TREK THROUGH COVA DELS COLOMS

START: ❶ Es Migjorn Gran	½ day
END: ❶ Es Migjorn Gran	Walking time
	(without stops)
Distance: easy	3 hours
🚶 12.5 km/7.8 mi ▪▫▫ Height: 140 m/459 ft	

COSTS: Approx. 20 euros for food
WHAT TO PACK: Protective footwear with good tread, snacks, drinking water, swimwear; torch or headlamp to explore the caves

IMPORTANT TIPS: Buses run in summer from Ferreries and Maó to Es Migjorn Gran.

One of the island's most beautiful walks through a gorge lined with holm oaks and pine trees to a stunning beach at the end. En route you will pass a cave which resembles a bizarre "cathedral" because of its stalactites. The route returns along a picturesque path slightly off the beaten track.

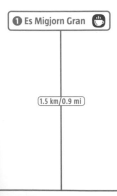

❶ Es Migjorn Gran ☕

1.5 km/0.9 mi

09:00am In ❶ **Es Migjorn Gran** → p. 71, treat yourself to a breakfast in the tapas bar INSIDER TIP **La Palmera** *(daily from 7am | C/ Major 83)*. **Then drive through the resort heading south-west towards the free car park near the cemetery. Then take the town's main road and turn left just before you leave the town into Camí de Sa Malagraba.** After leaving your car at the cemetery, **walk along the Camí de Binigaus Nou heading south.** To the right after 500 m/1640 ft the Binigaus Vell estate will come into view where the road trails off into a path behind the building. **Follow the path on your left signposted "Cova dels Coloms". Continue along the footpath**

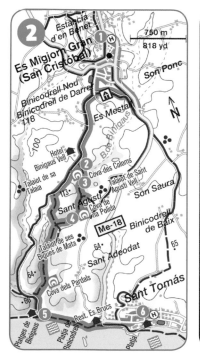

Gate to the underworld: Cova dels Coloms

through fields and down into the limestone gorge, the **② Barranc de Binigaus**. The landscape changes abruptly and the eroded limestone gorge fills with greenery. Aleppo pines, olive trees and holly oaks tower upwards with great northern divers and hoopoes fluttering in their branches.

Roughly halfway down to the sea, ignore the first left turn-off and, where the path forks after a short time, take the path straight on. You will soon come to the wide open mouth of the **③ Cova dels Coloms → p. 72** (doves' cave). The freely accessible cave owes its name to the hunting customs of previous generations. They stretched nets across the cave entrance to catch the doves nesting inside. In the thick layer of clay on the cave floor cult objects from Menorcan prehistory have also been found, suggesting that the wide hall was once used for ritual activities. Take a break to take in the vast size of the chamber towering 25 m/82 ft high and up to 110

② Barranc de Binigaus

250 m/820 ft

③ Cova dels Coloms

600 m/1969 ft

④ Cova Polida

2 km/1.25 mi

⑤ Platja de Binigaus

1 km/0.6 mi

⑥ Urbanització Sant Tomàs

7 km/4.3 mi

① Es Migjorn Gran

m/360 ft long. **Return to the main path at the bottom of the gorge and follow for a short distance. After five minutes you will reach a plateau where you take a path behind a gap in the wall heading left to the barranco. Turn left after 20 m/80 ft and then right up** to the entrance of the **④ Cova Polida** where you are unfortunately not allowed to enter to see the splendid stalactites due to the rare breed of bat which now resides inside. Once the ban is lifted again, you can admire beautiful stalagmites and stalagtites in the cave. **Having returned to the footpath, take the route down to the sea. When you reach a watering trough, take the signposted GR-223 path** where the gorge opens out into the **⑤ Platja de Binigaus** beach with its fine sands and turquoise sea, perfect for a spot of bathing.

12:00pm If you have forgotten to pack a picnic, you will find something to eat at **⑥ Urbanització Sant Tomàs To get there, follow the beach eastwards** to the beachside restaurant **Es Bruc → p. 72. To return to your car, walk to the end of the Platja de Binigaus and back along the same path to the watering trough. Then wander through the gorge until you reach the fork in the path after 10 minutes. Keep left and follow the cobblestone path** uphill past wild fruit trees and through wild, romantic scenery. **The path becomes wider, leading up to the Binigaus plain and back to the car park in ① Es Migjorn Gran.**

3 CYCLING ALONG THE NORTH COAST

START: ① Ferreries	1 Tag
END: ① Ferreries	Walking time 3 hours (10 km/6 mi), cycling time 3½ hours (40 km/25 mi)
Distance: very easy 🕐 50 km/31 mi Height: 100 m/328 ft	

COSTS: Approx. 15 euros for a trekking or mountain bike, 4.50 euros for entrance to the cheese museum, food in Es Mercadel 15–20 euros
WHAT TO PACK: swimwear, headwear, plenty of drinking water, comfortable shoes, picnic and bike lock (from the bike rental)

IMPORTANT TIPS: The first section of the bike route is extremely steep – you may have to push your bike for a few minutes.
The GR-223 hiking path is marked red.

Green hills and traditional villages, rugged coasts and picturesque bays: explore the island's highlights in the north on this combined trekking and cycling tour. The cycling tour takes you along tracks and tarmac roads, making it suitable for unexperienced cyclists as is the glorious clifftop walk with many nice views along a signposted path.

08:00am This route starts at the eastern outskirts of ❶ **Ferreries** → p. 67, to be precise at the petrol station in Polígono Industrial where you take the side road Camí de Sant Patrici heading north. A signpost points to the ❷ **Hort de Sant Patrici** → p. 68, where it's worth taking your first break: This historic estate is not only surrounded by beautiful gardens, it also houses an attractive **cheese**

❶ Ferreries

1.5 km/1 mi

❷ Hort de Sant Patrici

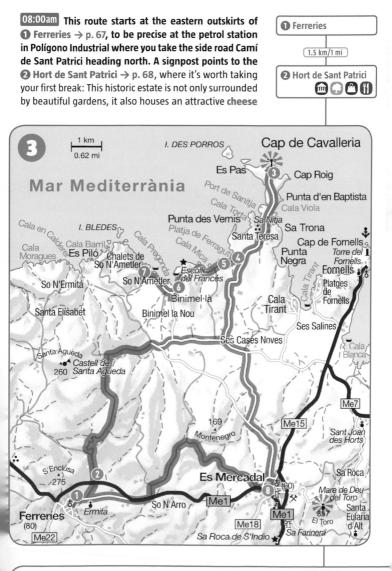

museum. Take a break here for a hearty snack because you'll soon have to pedal hard: **after the next fork in the road, keep right and cycle uphill (**19 percent gradient) – don't be disheartened, even the most conditioned bikers have to get off and push at this stage. Don't give up though because the hard work will be rewarded with fantastic 360° views at the **Son Pere Nou estate** with the fjord-like Fornells bay to the north, pine tree coasts to the south, the lagoon of S'Albufera des Grau to the east and green hills all around.

Before long the tarmac path ends **and takes a sharp left to the farmhouse of Sant Antoni. You should continue straight on though where you'll soon pass through an iron gate and then later on a wooden gate.** Continue cycling along this route with the Santa Águeda on your left, a castle built on the site of an ancient Arabian fortress which stands 260 m/853 ft above sea level. **Keep right at the next junction ignoring the entrance to the Son Rubí estate on your left.** You will now join a tarmac path which takes you over a bridge to a crossroads where you can go left to Binimel·là beach, and right to Es Mercadal. **You should continue straight on for a while until you reach the next large T-junction where you turn left. Continue along the tarmac stretch known as Camí des Far, or "lighthouse path" for a further 6 km/3.7 miles** – past the excavation site Ciutat Romana de Sanitja (currently not open to the public) – to the remotely situated ❸ **Cap de Cavalleria** → p. 57. Explore the area around the (no access) **lighthouse**! The side facing east where the cliffs look as if someone chipped away at them with an axe offers particularly spectacular views.

11:00am Then return along the road you took to the ❹ **car park (approx. 4 km/2.5 miles away)** where you will see the start of the hiking path signposted. Lock up your bike and head off on foot towards the coast. One of the path's highlights already awaits you at the start of your walk: climb down the steps to the ❺ **Platja de Cavalleria,**

Explore the island by bike

16 km/10 mi

❸ Cap de Cavalleria

4 km/2.5 mi

❹ car park

1 km/0.6 mi

❺ Platja de Cavalleria

a stunning double-crescent golden beach which is ideal for a spot of bathing! Then climb back up the steps and follow the picturesque coastal path to **⑥ Cala Binimel·là → p. 57**. This red sandy beach is also a perfect location to enjoy a swim. If you have worked up an appetite, head to the shady garden restaurant **Binimel·là** serving the best Menorcan cuisine. **Then follow the coastal path for another 20 minutes to ⑦ Cala Pregonda** with its bizarre rock formations. It's worth taking the same route back to the car park to enjoy the spectacular views.

03:00pm Now it's time to climb back on your bike **and cycle back southwards along the Camí des Far to the T-junction (approx. 3 km/1.9 mile away) where you bear left. After 1km/0.6mi shortly before reaching Ses Cases Noves, your route takes you right along another path through green plains. After 3 km/1.9 mile you'll reach another road** which you follow left back to **⑧ Es Mercadal → p. 58** Take a well-earned break in this "culinary paradise" – there are plenty of restaurants to choose from – before climbing on your bike again. **Now head west along the busy Me-1 for just 500 m/1640 ft, turning right down the** **INSIDER TIP** *Camí d'en Kane*. This narrow romantic road, named after the British governor who ordered its construction in the 18th century, takes you past farmhouses along a picturesque hilly landscape. **After just 6km/3.72mi it merges into the Me-1 which will bring you straight back to ⑥ Ferreries (a further 2 km/1.2 mile).**

4

UNSPOILT NATURE: HIKE IN ES GRAU

START: ⑥ Sa Mesquida	½ day
END: ⑥ Sa Mesquida	Walking time
	(without stops)
Distance: easy	approx. 4 ½ hours
🔁 17 km/11 mi ▫▪▪ Height: 350 m/1148 ft	

COSTS: Approx. 20 euros for food in Es Grau
WHAT TO PACK: Swimwear, headwear, plenty of drinking water, comfortable shoes, picnic, if you'd like

IMPORTANT TIPS: The starting point is only accessible by car. Other sections of the route are highlighted red along the GR-223 hiking path.

The wetlands of S'Albufera des Grau represent the centrepiece of Menorca's biosphere reserve – an ecosystem encompassing forests, meadows, marshes and lakes. The area is also home to ducks, geese, osprey and heron. This hiking tour takes you over several passes, along the coast and down to the area's vast freshwater lagoon. There is also time for a spot of bathing at a beach along the way.

❶ Sa Mesquida

2.3 km/1.4 mi

❷ Macar de Binillautí

1.2 km/0.7 mi

❸ Caleta de Binillautí

3 km/1.9 mi

❹ Punta de sa Gola

0.8 km/0.5 mi

❺ Platja d'Es Grau

1.2 km/0.7 mi

❻ Cala des Tamarells

2.5 km/1.6 mi

09:00am Starting from the car park at **❶ Sa Mesquida**, walk in the direction of the beach and keep left. At the end of the beach, the path leads up to the first pass and then descends down to the neighbouring bay of **❷ Macar de Binillautí** – *macar* is the term used in Menorca to describe a pebbly beach. **The path then ascends to a second pass and then down again to the bay of ❸ Caleta de Binillautí.** You pass through rugged scenery with bare rocks alternating with flat steppe landscape. **Shortly after leaving the bay, the path takes a turn inland, over another pass and along meadows to the Me-5. Follow it right and after 600 m/2000 ft follow the sign to the Lagune S'Albufera. Cross a canal over a bridge and keep left at the next junction (signpost: "Mirador" = viewpoint).** Follow the wooden walkways, which protect the salt-loving plants underneath, down to the lakeside where you can often spot heron and even osprey.

Now head up a flight of steps to the panoramic hill viewpoint **❹ Punta de sa Gola**, with the vast lagoon now at your feet: you are surrounded by hills behind you with the village of Es Grau nestled in the long bay stretching along the coast in front of you. **Climb down the steps and follow the walkway to the left.** The path leads you through a shady pine forest to the **❺ Platja d'Es Grau** dunes where you can bathe in the refreshing, turquoise waters.

At the north of the beach, the GR-223 signpost directs you inland through the pine forest. En route you will pass another panoramic viewpoint offering a fantastic sight of the slate black Cap de Favàritx and its lighthouse in the distance. The path then continues down to the **❻ Cala des Tamarells,** a bay dominated by the old watchtower **Torre de Rambla.** You can spend hours on this stranded Robinson Crusoe beach – it is the ideal spot for sunbathing, a refreshing swim in the sea and a picnic.

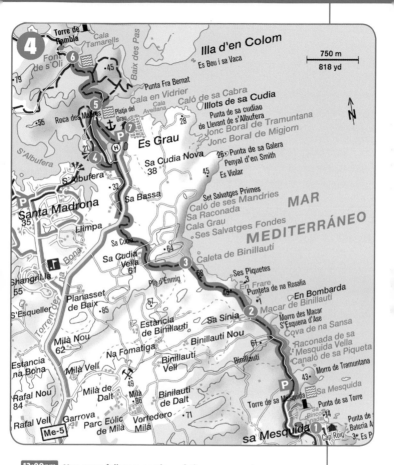

12:00pm You now follow a section of the same route back to the Platja des Grau. Take a well-earned break in the village of ❼ **Es Grau** → p. 58 located in the south.

INSIDER TIP ▶ **Bar Es Grau** *(daily 9.30am–10pm | Plaça de Mestre Jaume 13 |* Budget*)* € is a good choice serving delicious daily menus, salads or *bocadillos* on its delightful terrace. **From Es Grau follow the Me-5 for around 1.5 km/0.9 mile until you hit the red marked GR-223 on your left and can leave the tarmac road behind you.** You now return over hill and dale, back over the three passes, accompanied by beautiful scenery on your left and right back to ❶ **Sa Mesquida** where you started the tour.

❼ Es Grau

6.5 km/4 mi

❶ Sa Mesquida

SPORTS & ACTIVITIES

For Menorcans sport is part of everyday life and even small children are happy to go off on hikes and to go for a bathe at least once a week because from May to October the sea is ideal for swimming, and the mild Mediterranean climate encourages outdoor activities all year round.

All the larger towns and resorts have modern sport facilities such as sports halls, tennis courts and indoor pools, not to mention private fitness clubs. For holidaymakers there are sports facilities – such as tennis and volleyball courts, mini golf, bicycle hire and water sport schools – in their own holiday resort on the coast. The "Menorca Activa" brochure is useful: *www.menorcaactiva.com*. Those looking for good spa facilities need deeper pockets, because facilities can be found only in the four and five-star hotels.

CYCLING

Although Menorca at first sight appears flat, if you are not a fit and experienced cyclist you will soon feel the many ascents. The main roads are very busy, there are very few bicycle paths, and lots of minor roads are in a very poor condition. However, cycling can still be a real pleasure in certain areas. This includes the western and eastern parts of the island around Ciutadella and Maó. Bicycle and mountain bike hire is available in both towns and in almost all the holiday resorts.

If you prefer not to laze about on holiday, there is a lot on offer: swimming, horseback riding, tennis, golf, hiking and cycling

DIVING

The underwater world of Menorca is ideal for ★ *diving*, though it has to be said that the main attraction is not so much the richness of the marine life but rather the clear water which provides excellent visibility. There are also numerous underwater caves and lots of shipwrecks on the seabed. There are about 20 diving schools on the island. Trial sessions, a complete diver training programme and daily trips as well as the hire of diving equipment are all part of the standard range of diving centres in the main holiday resorts. Perhaps the nicest diving centre is: *Poseidon Diving School (in the Hostal Bahía | Cala Santandria | tel. 9 71 38 26 44 | www.bahia-poseidon.de/en/).*

GOLF

Menorca is not exactly a golfers' paradise because there is only one golf course on the island. The compact 18-hole course at *Son Parc (Urbanització Son Parc | Es Mercadal | enquiries and reservations: tel. 9 71 18 88 75 | www.golfsonparc.com*, despite its long and fast greens, is a relatively flat and easy course surrounded by lots of unspoilt nature. Only the 1st and the 9th holes are made a little challenging because of the terrain. The course is open all year round and you can also play tennis there, and there is a clubhouse with showers, bar and restaurant. The cheapest green fee is 39 euros (from 4pm) and a half hour lesson with the pro will cost approx. 40 euros.

HIKING & TREKKING

Many hotels have a ready supply of suggestions for walks for their guests. There are hiking trails all over the island, but they are rarely signposted and often blocked by walls, locked gates and thorny vegetation. Hiking or army maps (obtainable in bookshops) are very useful, but not always accurate. Hiking clubs and other institutions organise (usually in the off-peak seasons) hikes in which non-members can also participate (announcements in the daily press). The *Camí de Cavalls,* which encompasses the island, has been restored and signposted – check out online the many different places where you can join the trail: *www.camidecavalls360.com*.

Guided hikes are organised by *Dia complert (mobile tel. 6 09 67 09 96)*, *Viatges Magón (tel. 9 71 35 13 00 | www.menorcabookingcentre.com)* and *Xauxa Menorca Reloaded (C/ Verge del Toro 10 | Es Mercadal | mobile tel. 6 85 74 73 08 | www.rutasmenorca.com)*. The INSIDER TIP hikes through the gorges of the *Barranc d'Algendar (Club Aventura | Hotel Cala Galdana | tel. 9 71 15 45 00)* are really fantastic.

HORSEBACK RIDING

More than a dozen public and private riding schools (mostly in the island's interior) offer lessons and trail rides. There are also pony clubs for children. There are riding stables right on the coast in Cala en Bosc and a pony club in Sant Tomàs. Lists with addresses are available at the tourist information offices in Ciutadella and Maó.

The two racecourses *Hipódrom Municipal (Ctra. Maó–Sant Lluís | Sat 6pm in summer, Sun mornings in autumn)* and *Hipódrom Torre del Ram (Ciutadella | Urb. Torre del Ram | Sun 6pm),* organise trotting races every weekend.

SAILING

Sailing courses are offered in Fornells, Son Xoriguer and Maó. Larger yachts or sailing boats, also with a skipper, are available in the ports in Maó, Ciutadella, Fornells, Cala en Bosc and S'Algar. The best option is *Windsurf Fornells (mobile tel. 6 64 33 58 01 | www.windfornells.*

com). On presentation of a valid sailing licence, you can hire sailing yachts and motorboats in Maó, for example at *Nautic Fun (Moll de Llevant 57 | tel. 9 71 36 42 50 | www.nauticfunmenorca. com)*.

TENNIS

All the major hotels have their own courts and tennis coaches are usually also available. The public courts are also available to holidaymakers!

WATER SPORTS

In addition to diving, the other favourites are windsurfing and water skiing. Water skiing and paragliding are available in S'Algar and Cala en Bosc. Pedalos and smaller motorboats (without sailing licence) are available at most holiday beaches. You can hire kayaks and SUP surfboards in Cala Galdana, Son Xoriguer, Es Grau and Fornells. The latter in particular is great for voyages of discovery on the calm waters of the large INSIDER TIP bay of Fornells. For over twenty years, *Dia Complert* (see page 19) has been active here, with diving, kayak, flyboard and paddle surf excursions. *Surf & Sail* at the beach at *Son Xoriguer (mobile tel. 6 29 74 99 44 | www.surfsailmenorca. com)* has the widest range of offers.

WELLNESS

All of the newer four and five-star hotels offer spa facilities with massage pools, Jacuzzis as well as dry and wet saunas. These facilities are not always included in the price; you will always be charged extra for massages and treatments. The *Insotel Punta Prima Prestige (see p. 51)* offers the best spa on the island followed by *Barceló Pueblo Menorca (see p. 51)* in the same resort. The city hotels *Port Ciutadella (see p. 85)* and *Port Mahón (see p. 45)* are the perfect way to combine a wellness and culture break.

A well-maintained green at Son Parc golf course

TRAVEL WITH KIDS

Athough there are relatively few activities aimed at children part from the island's sand and sea, Menorca welcomes its young visitors with family-friendly services offered in most hotels. Many of the larger hotels and club sites are specially tailored for children. Childcare is provided and an entertainments team ensures games, sport and lots of fun activities.

However, outside the hotels child-centred facilities are rare and though you will find a playground in almost all public parks, you will look in vain for nappy changing facilities in restaurants. Most restaurants on the coast provide children's menus, and bicycles and hire cars can be rented with child seats. The small tourist trains, which are now in all the major holiday resorts, are an entertaining means of transport and the perfect way to explore your area.

There are special events for children on all the island's summer patron saint days, such as theatre, concerts, competitions and sport, which usually take place in the late afternoon. Gigantic papier maché puppets *(gigantes* and *capgrossos)* often parade through the resort afterwards. The festival programme is in the local newspaper on the day before the festival starts. Parts of the events include equestrian displays on the squares and in the narrow streets. But because of the crowds of people, these *jaleos* are not completely without their risks and you should avoid getting caught up in the throng, especially with small children and bug-

Water fun, horse rides and ancient ruins: on Menorca you can take your children with you everywhere – and most of them will love it!

gies. A better option are the *jaleos de ases* (processions with donkeys) in Ferreries and Es Migjorn Gran. Most children also enjoy being allowed to stay up late to watch the midnight firework displays. Boat tours can also make a very pleasant change, and there are trips along the coast with a break for a swim with the "Don Joan" from Port de Maó *(daily 10am, 2.30pm | see Maó, Sports & Activities)*. There are also swimming trips especially for youngsters from Cala en Bosc or all day tours with time on the beach from Ciutadella *(daily from 10am | information at the port)*.

MAÓ/EASTERN TIP

FORT MARLBOROUGH ★
(131 E–F4) (∅ K6)
Dark corridors, flickering candlelight, the thunder of cannons – with a light and sound show, the old British fortifications transport visitors back to the 18th century. **INSIDER TIP** Free admission on Mondays! From the parking lot, a long, shadeless

path leads to the fort, better to drive right up to the entrance! *June–Oct Mon–Tue 10am–3pm, Wed–Sun 9.30am–7.30pm, April/May, Nov/Dec Tue–Sat 9.30am–3pm, Jan–March closed | admission 3, children (8–16 years) 1.80 euros | Cala Sant Esteve (near Es Castell) | tel. 9 71 36 04 62*

MIGJORN/ISLAND CENTRE

CENTRE ARTESANAL DE MENORCA ●
(128 B3) (*ω F4*)

Es Mercadal has had a forum for artisans from all over the island since 2005. Here you can admire not only modern and traditional Menorcan craftsmanship in the form of calabash bottles, woven fabrics, pottery and ceramics, but you can also buy, if the fancy takes you. You can also watch the craftsmen at work, which is very interesting especially for children. After restoration work, the centre was reopened at the end of 2012 with a new arts and crafts gallery. *Mon–Fri 11am–2pm and 5–8pm, Sat 11am–2pm, March/April only in the morning, Nov–April closed | Av. del Metge Camps | Es Mercadal | tel. 9 71 15 36 44 | www.artesaniademenorca. com*

CENTRE DE LA NATURA DE MENORCA
(127 E4) (*ω E4*)

Small exhibition, presenting a different ecological topic each year, that has been designed with children mind. *May–Oct Tue–Sat 10.30am–1.30pm, 5.30pm–8pm, Sun 10.30am–1.30pm, Nov–April only Sat/Sun | admission 3 euros, children 2 euros | Camí des Castell 53 | Ferreries | www.gobmenorca.com*

CLUB SANT JAUME (128 B5–6) (*ω F5*)
The mini leisure park with pool and water slide, lawns for sunbathing – also with shaded areas and a café restaurant –

provides adults with peace and quiet and children with lots of fun. Next door is the Son Bou Laberinto. *May–Oct daily 10am–7pm | water park free admission | slide (2 ×) 1.50 euros, maze, games, entertainment 7.50 euros | Urbanització Sant Jaume*

ES LLOC DE MENORCA (128 C5) (*ω c5*)
At this small zoo near Alaior, children can visit kangaroos and emus, monkeys and lemurs as well as feed its goats, pigs and cows. *March–Nov. daily 10am–4pm | admission 11.50 euros, children up to 2 years free | Ctra. General, km 7.8 | www.llocde menorca.com*

SON MARTORELLET (127 E4) (*ω E4*)
New management of the stables has been a breath of fresh air. Fantastic equestrian shows are offered and you can also visit the stables themselves *(Mon, Wed, Fri 6pm–8pm). May–Oct 15-minute mini shows Wed–Thu 3.30pm, admission from 10.75 euros, children from 6.75 euros; evening shows Tue and Thu 8.30pm (June–Sept, on great demand also May and Oct), admission from 20 euros, children from 10 euros; tickets also online |Ctra. Cala Galdana, km 1.7 | tel. 9 71 373406 | www.sonmartorellet. com*

CIUTADELLA/WESTERN TIP

AQUA CENTER (126 A3) (*ω A3*)
Menorca's largest water park offers long water slides, an "adventure river", a "black hole", whirlpool, bouncy castle, playground equipment, restaurant, a go-kart track and a crèche for small children. *May–Oct daily 10.30am–6.30pm | admission 20 euros, children 10 euros | Urb. Los Delfines, north-west of Ciutadella | Av. Principal | www.aquacenter-menorca. com |*

AQUAROCK (126 B5) (*⬚ B5*)

The small water park in the south-west has water slides from *tube* to *kamikaze*, a wave pool, jacuzzi, children's pools and a large go-kart track right next door. *In summer daily (except on Sat in May, June and Sept) 10.30am–6pm | admission 20 euros, children 11, go-kart from 21 euros | Carreró Cova d'es Moro 88 | Cala en Bosc*

CAVALLS SON ÀNGEL ●
(126 C2) (*⬚ C3*)

Guided horse rides for the whole family through the unspoilt nature of the north coast are provided by *Toni Bosch*. The starting point is the neat, small estate *Finques Son Àngel* with friendly staff and relaxed atmosphere. Excursions take you through quiet nature reserves to the coast. *1 hr approx. 22 euros | getting there: Ciutadella, direction Cala Morell, then Camí d'Algaiarens "La Vall", km 1 | Toni Bosch mobile tel. 649 48 80 98 | www.cavallssonangel.com*

PEDRERA DE S'HOSTAL ★
(126 C3) (*⬚ C3*)

The half underground quarry museum near Ciutadella, developed out of an old limestone quarry, is an attractive place for exploring, picnics and games of hide and seek. A labyrinth of limestone blocks has been created especially for children. *Daily 9.30am–2.30pm, May–Sept also Mon–Sat 4.30pm to sunset | admission 4 euros, children free | Camí vell, km 1 | Ciutadella | www.lithica.es*

SURF & SAIL
(126 B5) (*⬚ B5*)

Learn how to sail or windsurf, how to glide over the waves on water skis or have fun on the water banana – and not just for adults: there are special courses for children too. *Son Xoriguer | tel. 9 71 38 72 85 | tel. 9 71 38 71 05 | www.surfsailmenorca.com*

Fun in the sun: a slide into some cool water

FESTIVALS & EVENTS

Actually it is said that the Menorcans, by Mediterranean standards, are rather restrained in character. But this is refuted every year in June when the St John festival in Ciutadella is a highlight of the festival calendar. Horses dash through the crowds, there is lots of laughter, dancing, flirting and drinking.

LOCAL FESTIVALS & EVENTS

MARCH/APRIL
Setmana Santa (Holy Week); Good Friday procession in Maó; on Easter Sunday choirs perform all over the island

APRIL
23: *Festa de Sant Jordi* (St George's Day); roses and books are sold on the market squares

MAY
8: *Festa de la Verge del Toro*; as the island's patron saint, the Holy Virgin of Monte Toro is venerated

MAY/JUNE
Pentecostés (Whitsuntide); trips into the countryside are typical, often combined with a family picnic

JUNE
INSIDERTIP *Diumenge des Be* (Sunday of the Sheep); the St John celebrations are launched with a procession of sheep. 23/24: ★ *Festes de Sant Joan*; highlight of the festival week with cavalcades *(caragols)*, concerts and fireworks.
29: *Festa de Sant Pere*; fishing festival with sailing regattas at Port de Maó

JULY
15/16: *Festa del Carme* in Maó, Ciutadella, Fornells; boat processions in honour of Our Lady of Mount Carmel
24/25, Es Castell: *Festa de Sant Jaume* in honour of St James with cavalcades, music and firework display at the port
3rd Sun, Es Mercadal: *Festa de Sant Martí* in honour of St Martin with processions and cavalcade
End July–end Aug: *Matins de l'orgue*; free organ recitals in Maó in the Santa María church; additionally the *Festival de Música de Maó*; *festivaldemusicademao. com*

AUGUST
9 Aug–beginning of Sept: **INSIDERTIP** *Festival de Música d'Estiu* (summer music festival) held in the seminary in Ciutadella and an even more spectacu-

**Quiet and restrained? No chance!
The many exuberant patron saints festivals
with cavalcades are typical of Menorca**

lar venue just outside the city, the former quarry *L'Hostal de Líthica*

First weekend, Es Migjorn Gran: ***Festa de Sant Cristófol*** in honour of St Christopher

2nd weekend, Alaior: ***Festes de Sant Llorenç*** in honour of St Lawrence; horse races, procession

3rd weekend, Sant Climent: ***Festes de Sant Climent*** in honour of St Clement, water fights, cavalcade

23–25, Ferreries: ***Festes de Sant Bartomeu*** in honour of St Bartholomew; cavalcades, fun fair

4th weekend, Sant Lluís: ***Festes de Sant Lluís*** in honour of St Louis, with floats, concerts, fun fair, fireworks

SEPTEMBER

7–9, Maó: ***Festes de la Verge de Gràcia*** in honour of the capital's patron saint, with street parties, equestrian displays, medieval markets, fun fair and fireworks

Sept/Oct in Maó and Ciutadella: ***Festival de Jazz*** with international stars

NATIONAL HOLIDAYS

1 January	*Cap d'any,* New Year
6 January	*Tres Reis,* Epiphanye
17 January	*Festa de Sant Antonii*
1 March	*Dia de les Illes Balears,* Balearics Day
March/April	Maundy Thursday; Good Friday
1 May	*Festa de Treball,* Labour Day
15 August	*L'Assumpció,* Assumption
2 October	*Dia de l'Hispanitat,* Discovery of America
1 November	*Tots Sants,* All Saints' Day
6 December	*Dia de la Constitució,* Contitutio Day
8 December	*La Immaculada Concepció,* Immaculate Conception
25/26 Dec	*Nadal,* Christmas

LINKS, BLOGS, APPS & MORE

LINKS & BLOGS

menorca-live.com This site calls itself the "essential online guide to island life", and with good reason. It contains a wealth of information with lots of suggestions what to do and the latest news about events on the island

www.visitmenorca.com The official site of the Menorca Hotel Association and it provides lots of other useful information

menorcadiferente.com/mapas-de-menorca Excellent collection of useful maps including an overview of the nature reserves and the hiking trails along the *Camí de Cavalls*

www.gobmenorca.com Official site of the environment protection group GOB *(Grup Balear d'Ornitologia)*. It may well contain lots of interesting information, but be aware that the English version has been created by Google translate and it is perhaps more worth reading for its hilarious English!

www.elpaladar.es On this website you can order typical Menorcan products such as wine or cheese online, but be aware that the site is completely in Spanish!

www.beautybyanya.com A new business model that provides mobile beauty treatments from pedicures to facials and various massages: you can enjoy the treatment on the spot in every resort on the island – even in your hotel and on Sundays and public holidays

toniponsbarro.blogspot.com Very nice blog with professional photographs and background music. Unfortunately only in Spanish, but nonetheless highly recommended

www.menorcaminorca.co.uk Colourful site with a mix of blog and information, tips on cheap flights, accommodation, sports opportunities, Spanish lessons and lots more

www.museudemenorca.com/en/blog Blog by the island museum with inte-

Regardless of whether you are still preparing your trip or already on Menorca: these addresses will provide you with more information, videos and networks to make your holiday even more enjoyable

resting news concerning archaeological finds and the like

www.facebook.com/menorca Usual Facebook site where you can get the latest news, look at photos and swap opinions

VIDEOS

www.pbase.com/jserranog/menorca Lots of atmospheric photos and impressions by Jaime Serrano, who knows the island really well

fotomenorca.blogspot.com Cheeky photo blog by Sergio Vargas, with lots of unusual motifs and outstanding photos (also black and white)

www.youtube.com/watch?v=Pm2DBpm-xZ4&feature=related Interesting professional 20-minute video *Menorca desde el cielo* providing a bird's eye view of Menorca, but commentary only in Spanish

flickrhivemind.net/Tags/menorca,underwater/Interesting Word has got round that Menorca also has lots of underwater attractions. If you don't believe it, have a look here

APPS

Menorca Offline Maps Good maps which can be used offline with GPS link for iPhone etc.

Cami de Cavalls This app shows you some of the nicest hiking trails on the island, among them the eponymous horse trail

Menorca Beach A beach guide to all the hot spots of the beach scene

Meet up Use this app to arrange hikes, concert outings and boat trips with like-minded individuals

TRAVEL TIPS

ARRIVAL

Menorca is only about a two-hour flight away from all the major airports in central Europe. The best deals are those offered by charter flights, with or without a complete package, as well as part of special offers from the major tour organisers. But there are also scheduled flights (amongst others, Condor direct, Iberia or – much cheaper – its no-frills carrier Vueling via Barcelona) connecting the European mainland with the Aeroport de Menorca (5 km/3.1 miles southwest of Maó). Direct flights from the UK are available with *Monarch (www. monarch.co.uk), easyJet (www.easyjet. com), Ryanair (www.ryanair.com)* and *Jet 2 (jet2.com).* From the airport you can get a bus, but most tour operators have their own transfer networks between the airport and the hotels.

Travelling from France is best via the A7 Dijon–Lyon–Nîmes motorway through the Rhone Valley, then on the A9 to Perpignan, crossing into Spain at Figueres and then by ferry from Barcelona or València. Motorways in France and Spain are subject to charges.

Ferries sail from Barcelona and València several times a week, in summer more frequently, and their destination is Port de Maó *(approx. 8 hours)*. You can also use the cheap flights to neighbouring Mallorca and then take the Maó–Palma ferry *(only Sat/Sun, 6–7 hours | Trasmediterránea-Acciona | Maó | Moll Comercial | tel. 9 02 45 46 45 | www. trasmediterranea.es)*. Other connections: Alcúdia–Ciutadella *(approx. 3 hours | Iscomar | tel. 9 02 11 91 28 or from abroad 0034 9 71 43 75 00 | wwwiscomar.com)*, Alcúdia–Ciutadella/Maó *(fast car ferry | Baleària | tel. 9 02 16 01 80 | www.balea ria.com)*. Reservations are recommended in the summer season (May–Oct), especially if you're travelling by car from the mainland.

RESPONSIBLE TRAVEL

It doesn't take a lot to be environmentally friendly whilst travelling. Don't just think about your carbon footprint whilst flying to and from your holiday destination but also about how you can protect nature and culture abroad. As a tourist it is especially important to respect nature, look out for local products, cycle instead of driving, save water and much more. If you would like to find out more about eco-tourism please visit: *www.ecotourism.org*

BANKS & CREDIT CARDS

Banks are usually only open 9am–1pm or 2pm, but bureaux de change in the tourist resorts are often open in the afternoon. There are numerous ATMs and credit cards are widely used and are accepted in almost all shops, hotels and restaurants. Card providers with the most extensive network on the island are VISA, Mastercard and Eurocard; American Express and Diners Club are not as yet widely accepted.

From arrival to weather

BUSES

The public transport network is dominated by three companies: *TMSA (tel. 9 71 36 04 75 | www.tmsa.es)*, *Autos Fornells (mobile tel. 6 86 93 92 46 | www.autofornells.com)* and *Torres (tel. 9 71 38 64 61 | www.bus.e-torres.net)*. The current bus timetables for the Maó area and to the airport are on the internet at *www.menorca.tib.org*.

CAMPING

To find out whether or not camping is allowed, you need to check with the municipality or the respective property owner. Camping rough is prohibited as is camping in the nature reserves! There are two campsites: *S'Atalaia (May–Oct | Ferreries –Cala Galdana, km 4 | tel. 9 71 37 42 32 | www.campingsatalaia.com)*, 3 km/2 miles from the coast, in a pine forest between Ferreries and Cala Galdana, and *Son Bou (April–Oct | Ctra. de San Jaume, km 3.5 | tel. 9 71 37 27 27 | www.campingsonbou.com)* which has lots of opportunities for sport.

CAR

If not otherwise signposted, the maximum speed limit in built up areas is 50 km/30 mph, on main roads 80 km/50 mph but if there is a hard shoulder at least 1.5m wide, then 100 km/60 mph. Seatbelts are obligatory for both the front seat passenger and back seat passenger (if belts are fitted in the rear). Wearing a helmet is obligatory for moped and motorbike riders. Motorists must carry two reflective vests and two warning triangles

BUDGETING

Coffee	£1.20–£2/$1.8–$3 *for a latte in a café*
Menorcan cheese	£8–£13/$11–$19 *per kilo in a shop*
Wine	£7–£14/$10–$21 *for a bottle in a restaurant*
Abarques	£13–£24/$20–$36 *for a pair of typical Menorcan sandals*
Fuel	around £1.3/$2 *for a litre of super*
Disco	£13–£21/$20–$33 *admission in the evening*

in case of accident or breakdown; the use of a mobile phone without hands-free facility is strictly prohibited. And breathalyser tests are carried out more frequently; the drink drive limit is *0.5*.

People drive in Menorca with a certain Mediterranean nonchalance. This is particularly evident at pedestrian crossings which are largely ignored and at traffic lights where people are happy to race through on amber/red.

Super, diesel and lead free *(sin plomo)* and also Super or Extra lead free (98 octane) are available at eleven filling stations: in Maó (3), Ciutadella (3), Alaior (2), Sant Lluís, Es Mercadal and on the main Maó–Fornells road.

CAR AND (MOTOR)CYCLE HIRE

You can hire a car at the airport and in all the major tourist resorts. You will find bicycles in almost all the holiday resorts, but motorcycles only in Ciutadella and Maó. Price comparisons are worthwhile; the most expensive car rentals are at the airport. You can hire a Twingo for 25–40 euros per day, a Peugeot 206 or Renault Megane for 33–53 euros/day, including insurance. Find car hire deals at *www.autosmenorca.com, www.autosmaximo.com* or *www.binicars-menorca.com*. Rental listings for cars, small motorcycles and bicycles in Maó at *Autos Mahon Rent (Moll de Llevant 35–36 | tel. 9 71 36 56 66 | www.autosmahonrent.com)*. You can hire bicycles (from mountain bikes to road-racers) at *Bike Menorca (www.bike-menorca.com)* in Ciutadella *(Plaça Menorca)* and in Maó *(Av. Francesc Femenías 44)*.

CONSULATES & EMBASSIES

UK HONORARY VICE CONSULATE
Cami Biniatap, 32 | Horizonte | tel. +34 971 36 33 73 | Mon–Fri 10am–midday

US CONSULATE
There is no consulate on Menorca, but there is one on Mallorca: *c/Porto Pi, 8, Edif Reina Constanza 9A | Palma de Mallorca | tel. +34 971 40 37 07 | Mon–Fri 10.30am–1.30pm | madrid.usembassy.gov/citizen-services/offices/mallorca.html*

CUSTOMS

For EU citizens the following duty free allowances apply (import and export): for own consumption 800 cigarettes, 400 cigarillos, 200 cigars, 1kg tobacco, 20L aperitif, 90L wine (with a maximum amount of 60L sparkling wine) and 110L beer.
Travellers to the US who are residents of the country do not have to pay duty on articles purchased overseas up to the value of $800, but there are limits on the amount of alcoholic beverages and tobacco products. For the regulations for international travel for US residents please see *www.cbp.gov*

ELECTRICITY

The mains voltage in all hotels and hostels is 220 volts, but British electrical items will work with the correct travel plug adaptor to convert the UK standard 3 pin to Spanish 2 pin socket. North American visitors should also bring a transformer.

EMERGENCIES

In an emergency, phone *112* whatever the problem. This service is also available in English. If you lose your bank or credit card, contact your bank in the UK immediately and report the theft to the police. Make sure you have made a note of your card company's 24-hour contact phone number before you go away. If your cards are registered with a card protection agency, ensure you have their contact number and your policy number with you.

HEALTH

Chemists *(farmacias)* are indicated with a green cross – usually as a neon light. When closed, a notice displays the nearest emergency chemist.
In the case of illness, the EHIC (European Health Insurance Card) card is valid. American visitors are advised to ensure they have health insurance. Medical services often have to be paid for in cash, in which case it is important to get a receipt *(recibo oficial)* from the doctor (also for expensive medicines or dental treatment) so that you can be reimbursed.

In the holiday resorts there are special *centros médicos* which are equipped to deal with medical needs, communication problems and the most common holiday illnesses. Dentists are listed under *dentista*. You can call for an ambulance day and night on *tel. 061*.

information: *www.menorca.es, www. tourspain.es, www.visitmenorca.com, www.visitbalears.com* or from the call centre: tel. *9 71 35 59 52*

If you speak Spanish, this social media platform allows locals and tourists to have their say: *www.menorca.info.*

IMMIGRATION

Visitors from Britain will need a valid passport – even though it is no longer checked on immigration from Schengen countries – and should have it on you at all times in the case of police checks (for motorists), when notifying a theft etc. Tourists from America, Canada and Australia do not need a visa for stays under 90 days.

INFORMATION

SPANISH TOURIST OFFICE TURESPAÑA
– *64 North Row | W1K 7DE, London | tel. 020 7317 2011 | www.spain.info*
– *845 North Michigan Av, Suite 915-E | Chicago IL 60611 | tel. 312 642 1992 | www. spain.info/en_US*
– *20 East 42nd Street, Suite 5300 | New York NY 10165-0039 | tel. 216 265 8822 | www.spain.info/en_US*

OFICINA DE INFORMACIÓN TURÍSTICA
– *Maó (Plaça Constitució 22 | tel. 9 71 35 59 52)*
– *Ciutadella (Plaça d'es Born 15 | tel. 9 71 48 41 55)*
You can get on the spot assistance and information not only at the two tourist offices in Maó and Ciutadella, but also at the information booth at the airport *(arrivals hall | only in the summer)*, the office at the Port de Maó *(Moll de Llevant 2 | tel. 9 71 35 59 52)* as well as a mobile support office which visits the main resorts for one day each in summer. General

INTERNET & WIFI

The island's government launched a free ● 30-minute WiFi service accessible in all larger resorts. A free Internet service will also soon be available on all the island's beaches! Log on to the Internet at *www.menorcawifi.com* where online access costs approx. 5 euros for a day. Many bars (usually cafés) and hotels (nearly always in the reception area) have also set up small W-Fi zones where visitors have to ask at the reception or the restaurant owner for the access code: "Cual es la clave de la red inalambrica?" You will be charged for use more frequently here than on the Spanish mainland (3–6 euros a day). Your travel operator or porter can provide more information.

Internet cafés are few and far between. There is one in Ciutadella *(Plaça des Pins 37)*, one in Maó *(C/ Nou 25)* and one in Es Mercadal *(Av. Mestre Gari 48)*.

LANGUAGE

You can get by quite well on Menorca with English, but Spanish *(castellano)* is, of course, even better. If you'd like to surprise your host with a few words in *català*, you will find a few expressions in the "Useful Phrases", p. 120. But remember that there are some differences between the *menorquí* dialect and Catalan.

CURRENCY CONVERTER

£	€	€	£
1	1.17	1	0.85
3	3.50	3	2.56
5	5.86	5	4.26
13	15.24	13	11.09
40	47	40	34.11
75	88	75	63.96
120	141	120	102
250	293	250	213
500	586	500	426

$	€	€	$
1	0.94	1	1.06
3	2.82	3	3.19
5	4.70	5	5.32
13	12.22	13	13.83
40	37.60	40	42.55
75	70.50	75	79.78
120	113	120	128
250	235	250	266
500	470	500	532

For current exchange rates see www.xe.com

PHONE & MOBILE PHONE

The international dialling code for Spain is *+34*, followed by the 9-digit number. For the UK *+44* and for the US and Canada *+1*. You can phone home from every telephone booth which is marked *internacional*. The cabins also accept the practical telephone cards, *teletarjeta,* which are sold at newspaper kiosks. In telephone and Internet shops *(locutorios)* you will be charged at the end of your call.

However there are no restrictions on the use of mobile phones on the island. If you plan to phone a lot while you're on Menorca and want to avoid paying high roaming fees, you are advised to buy a pre-paid card and use it instead of your UK SIM card while on the island so that calls can be accepted for free. Pre-paid cards are available from tobacconists and newsagents, kiosks, supermarkets and petrol stations. The largest operators on the island are *Orange, Movistar* and *Telefónica.* All you need to purchase a card is a valid passport or personal ID card.

NEWSPAPERS

All the important mass circulation English daily and weekend newspapers as well as magazines are available on Menorca, but usually with one or two days delay. There is no English newspaper especially for holidaymakers such as is available on Mallorca and Ibiza.

NUDIST BEACHES

In contrast to the other Balearic islands, Menorca has no designated nudist beaches. But topless bathing is tolerated on all beaches and in small, hidden away bays people also sunbathe in the nude.

POST

Postage for letters (up to 20 g) and postcards to the rest of Europe is currently 90 cents. You can buy stamps at the post office and in all the tobacconists identified with the national colours; post offices are only open in the mornings (in Maó all day). The main post offices are: *Alaior (C/ Forn 1), Es Castell (C/ Llevant), Ciutadella (Pl. des Born 5), Maó (C/ Bonaire 15).*

PRICES

Compared with prices on the mainland, those on the island are a little higher, especially for lots of foodstuffs. The admission fee for museums is between 3–6 euros, the set menu in an average restaurant costs 15–30 euros.

Should there be no taxi waiting there, the taxi headquarters will help. *Maó: tel. 9 71 36 71 11 | Ciutadella: tel. 9 71 48 22 22*

RADIO

Radio One Mallorca is a 24-hour English radio station with lots of news, events, fiestas, local personalities and more. Though based in Mallorca, it also promotes events on Menorca and is available via radio (97.7 FM on Menorca), on the internet and via mobile phones. *www.radioonemallorca. com*

TAXIS

You can find taxis even in the smaller towns, usually at a designated taxi rank.

TELEVISION

Almost all the hotels have satellite dishes and receive programmes in English.

TIPPING

The Spanish themselves are not big tippers. The rule of thumb when tipping waiters in restaurants is: small change to round off the bill for a simple meal, 5–10 percent of the total bill for a more elaborate one. Room maids, porters, taxi drivers and guides are also pleased when they receive a tip.

WEATHER IN MAÓ

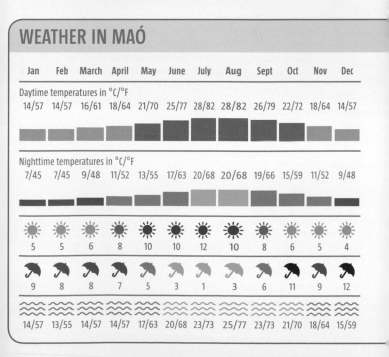

	Jan	Feb	March	April	May	June	July	Aug	Sept	Oct	Nov	Dec
Daytime temperatures in °C/°F	14/57	14/57	16/61	18/64	21/70	25/77	28/82	28/82	26/79	22/72	18/64	14/57
Nighttime temperatures in °C/°F	7/45	7/45	9/48	11/52	13/55	17/63	20/68	20/68	19/66	15/59	11/52	9/48
Sunshine hours/day	5	5	6	8	10	10	12	10	8	6	5	4
Precipitation days/month	9	8	8	7	5	3	1	3	6	11	9	12
Water temperature in °C/°F	14/57	13/55	14/57	14/57	17/63	20/68	23/73	25/77	23/73	21/70	18/64	15/59

☀ Sunshine hours/day　🌂 Precipitation days/month　≈≈ Water temperature in °C/°F

USEFUL PHRASES CATALAN

PRONUNCIATION

c	like "s" before "e" and "i" (e.g. Barcelona); like "k" before "a", "o" and "u" (e.g. Casa)
ç	pronounced like "s" (e.g. França)
g	like "s" in "pleasure" before "e" and "i"; like "g" in "get" before "a", "o" and "u"
l·l	pronounced like "l"
que/qui	the "u" is always silent, so "qu" sounds like "k" (e.g. perquè)
v	at the start of a word and after consonants like "b" (e.g. València)
x	like "sh" (e.g. Xina)

IN BRIEF

Yes/No/Maybe	Sí/No/Potser
Please/Thank you/Sorry	Sisplau/Gràcies/ Perdoni
May I...?	Puc ...?
Pardon?	Com diu *(Sie)*?/Com dius *(Du)*?
I would like to.../	Voldria.../
Have you got...?	Té...?
How much is...?	Quant val...?
I (don't) like this	(no) m'agrada
good	bo/bé *(Adverb)*
bad	dolent/malament *(Adverb)*
Help!/Attention!/Caution!	Ajuda!/Compte!/Cura!
ambulance	ambulància
police/fire brigade	policia/bombers
Prohibition/forbidden	prohibició/prohibit
danger/dangerous	perill/perillós
May I take a photo here/of you?	Puc fer-li una foto aquí?

GREETINGS, FAREWELL

Good morning!/afternoon!	Bon dia!
Good evening!/night!	Bona tarda!/Bona nit!
Hello!/Goodbye!	Hola!/Adéu! Passi-ho bé!
See you	Adéu!
My name is...	Em dic...
What's your name?	Com es diu?

Parles Català?

"Do you speak Catalan?" This guide will help you to say the basic words and phrases in Catalan

DATE & TIME

Monday/Tuesday	dilluns/dimarts
Wednesday/Thursday	dimecres/dijous
Friday/Saturday	divendres/dissabte
Sunday/working day	diumenge/dia laborable
holiday	dia festiu
today/tomorrow/	avui/demà/
yesterday	ahir
hour/minute	hora/minut
day/night/week	dia/nit/setmana

TRAVEL

open/closed	obert/tancat
entrance/driveway	entrada
exit/exit	sortida
departure/	sortida/
departure/arrival	sortida d'avió/arribada
toilets/restrooms /	Lavabos/
ladies/gentlemen	Dones/Homes
Where is...?/	On està...?/
Where are...?	On estan...?
left/right	a l'esquerra/a la dreta
close/far	a prop/lluny
bus	bus
taxi/cab	taxi
bus stop/	parada/
cab stand	parada de taxis
parking lot/	aparcament/
parking garage	garatge
street map/map	pla de la ciutat/mapa
train station/harbour	estació/port
airport	aeroport
schedule/ticket	horario/bitllet
train / platform/track	tren/via
platform	andana
I would like to rent...	Voldria llogar...
a car/a bicycle	un cotxe/una bicicleta
petrol/gas station	gasolinera
petrol/gas / diesel	gasolina/gasoil
breakdown/repair shop	avaria/taller

FOOD & DRINK

Could you please book a table for tonight for four?	Voldriem reservar una taula per a quatre persones per avui al vespre
on the terrace	a la terrassa
The menu, please	la carta, sisplau
Could I please have...?	Podria portar-me...?
bottle/carafe/glass	ampolla/garrafa/got
salt/pepper/sugar	sal/pebrot/sucre
vinegar/oil	vinagre/oli
vegetarian/	vegetarià/vegetariana/
allergy	allèrgia
May I have the bill, please?	El compte, sisplau

SHOPPING

Where can I find...?	On hi ha...?
I'd like.../	voldria/
I'm looking for...	estic buscant...
pharmacy/chemist	farmacia/drogueria
baker/market	forn/mercat
shopping center	centre comercial/gran magatzem
supermarket	supermercat
kiosk	quiosc
expensive/cheap/price	car/barat/preu
organically grown	de cultiu ecológic

ACCOMMODATION

I have booked a room	He reservat una habitació
Do you have any... left?	Encara té...
single room	una habitació individual
double room	una habitació doble
breakfast/half board	esmorzar/mitja pensió
full board	pensió completa
at the front/seafront	exterior/amb vistes al mar
shower/sit down bath	dutxa/bany
balcony/terrace	balcó/terrassa

BANKS, MONEY & CREDIT CARDS

bank/ATM	banc/caixer automàtic
pin code	codi secret
cash/	al comptat/
credit card	amb targeta de crèdit
change	canvi

HEALTH

doctor/dentist/paediatrician	metge/dentista/pediatre
hospital/emergency clinic	hospital/urgència
fever/pain	febre/dolor
inflamed/injured	inflamat/ferit
plaster/bandage	tireta/embenat
ointment/cream	pomada/crema
pain reliever/tablet	analgèsic/pastilla

POST, TELECOMMUNICATIONS & MEDIA

stamp/letter/postcard	segell/carta/ postal
I need a landline phone card	Necessito una targeta telefònica per la xarxa fixa
I'm looking for a prepaid card for my mobile	Estic buscant una targeta de prepagament pel mòbil
Where can I find internet access?	On em puc connectar a Internet?
Do I need a special area code?	He de marcar algun prefix determinat?
socket/adapter/charger	endoll/adaptador/carregador
computer/battery/ rechargeable battery	ordinador/bateria/ acumulador
at sign (@)	arrova
internet address	adreça d'internet (URL)
e-mail address	adreça de correu electrònic
e-mail/file/print	correu electrònic/fitxer/imprimir

LEISURE, SPORTS & BEACH

beach	platja
sunshade/lounger	para-sol/gandula

NUMBERS

0	zero	12	dotze	60	seixanta
1	un/una	13	tretze	70	setanta
2	dos/dues	14	catorze	80	vuitanta
3	tres	15	quinze	90	noranta
4	quatre	16	setze	100	cent
5	cinc	17	disset	200	dos-cents/dues-centes
6	sis	18	divuit	1000	mil
7	set	19	dinou	2000	dos mil
8	vuit	20	vint	10000	deu mil
9	nou	30	trenta		
10	deu	40	quaranta	½	mig
11	onze	50	cinquanta	¼	un quart

ROAD ATLAS

The green line indicates the Discovery Tour "Menorca at a glance"
The blue line indicates the other Discovery Tours

All tours are also marked on the pull-out map

Photo: Cows in the island's interior

Exploring Menorca

The map on the back cover shows how the area has been sub-divided

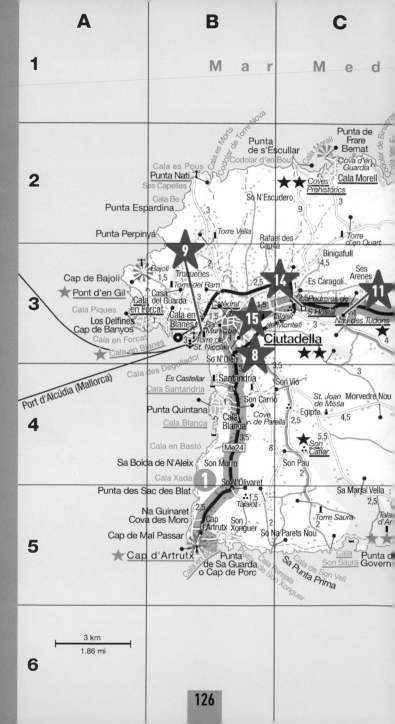

D

E

F

terrània

I. DES PORROS

Es Pas

1

Cap Gros

Racó des Llenyam

Cala en Carbó

ta Rotja

Port de Sanitja

Cala Torta

Punta des Vernís

Sa

Port de Ferragut

Platja de Ferragut

Cala en Caldera

I. BLEDES

Santa Te

Sa Falconera

Cala Moragues

Cala del Pilar

Cala Barril

Es Piló

Chalets de So N'Ametler

Platja de Ferragut

Cala Mica

Escollo dell'Francès

2

Sa Muntanya Mala 205

La Vall

So N'Ermità

So N'Ametler

Binimel·là

Santa Elisabet

3 Binimel la Nou

Sant Felip

4,5

Ses Cases N

2,5

Sa Font Santa

Santa Agueda

4,5

S'Almudaina

Castell de Santa Agueda 260

3

5,5

3

Son Planes

Alqueria Blanca

1

bre

Binisues □ 3,5

169

3

Montenegro

1

Ses Tavernes

191

27

Son Sintes

Santa Bárbara

3,5

3

Es Mercadal

Clafuda

Son Toni Martí

Torre Trencada

S'Enclusa 275

7,5

So N'Arro

Me1

orre Trencada

Pas d'En Revull

Ferreries

(80) 2

Ermita

Me18

Sa Roca

Torre Petxina

Barranc d'Algendar

Macarella

Naveta

7

Ses Fontsredones 237 3

4,5

4

Me22

4,5

Me16

4,5

Santa Ponça

Migjorn Gran

Es Migjorn Gran

Santa Ana

1

Son Mercer de Baix

(111)

Cala Santa Galdana

Binicudrell

Me18

10

Serpentona

7

1,5

Cova dels Coloms

5

S'Enfonsat de Binisaid

Cala Mitjana

Cova Polida

Sant Agustí

5

Torre Soli

136

rjal va

Cala Macarella

Cala Santa Galdana

Cala Trebalúger

Cala Mitjana

2

Sant Adeodat

Sant Tomás

Sant Jaume Mediterrani

en eta

Cala Escorxada

Punta Rabiosa

Platja Sant Tomás

1,5

Sant

Punta Negra

Platges de Son Bou

Punta d'Atalitx

Son Bou

Bas Palí San

Cap de ses Penyes

Cala de Llucalari

5

Cala de St. Llo

6

A **B** **C**

Barcelona

1

I. DES PORROS
Es Pas
3
12
Cap de Cavalleria ★★
Cap Roig
Port de Sanitja
Cala Tirant
Punta d'en Baptista
Cala Viola
Punta des Vernis
Sa Nitja
Na Guillemass
Platja de Ferragut
Cala Mica
Santa Teresa
Sa Trona
Cova dels Angle
BLEDES
Barril
Piló
Cala Presonda
Punta Negra
Cap de Fornells
122
Cova Polida
Morro de
Chalets de
So N'Ametler
Escullo
del Francés
Torre del
Fornells
Fornells
Punta
Badia
Coves Neg
So N'Ametier
Binimel·la
Cala
Tirant
Platges
de
Fornells
2.5
Es Niu de
3 Binimel la Nou
I. RAVELLS
de
Cala Pudent
Arenal de So
Ses Cases Noves
Ses Salines
2,5
Fornells
Cap de
Arenal
d'en
Castell
stell de
nta Agueda
Cala
Blanca
10
1,5
Son Parc
★
5,5
3
2,5
Arenal
d'en Castell
3
2
Me7
1,5
3
169
Me15
7
Sant Joan
des Horts
1
Ses
Coves
Velles
102
Cala
Montenegro
Llucaitx
Ses
Cove
3,5
Me9
3
2,3
Es Mercadal
★
(60)
4
Sa Roca
4
Hort de
Llucaitx
Bin
7,5
Mare de Déu
del Toro
So N'Arro
Me1
357
El Toro
Santa Eularia
d'Alt
Puig de S'Albaida
Ermita
Me18
Sa farinera
172
Naveta
Sa Roca de S'Indio
6
Camí d'en Kane
S'Albaida
7
7
Ses Fontsredones
237
3
Son Gall
Migjorn Gran
er
4,5
4,5
Me1
S'Artiga Vella
San
de E
Es Migjorn
Gran
Me16
Coves de
S'Encantament
(111)
Cementiri
Binicudrell
1,5
Me18
Cova dels
Coloms
2
1
1
(130)
1,5
Alaior
★
va Polida
3
1,5
Sant Agustí
Llucassaldent
5
Sant Adeodat
5
2,5
24
Sant Tomás
La Argenti
5,5
a Sant Tomás
Torre Soll
136
1,5
Punta Negra
1,5
Sant Jaume
Mediterrani
★★
Torralba
d'en Salort
Punta d'Atalitx
4,5
Sant Jaume
Torre
d'en Galmés
★★
6
Platges de Son Bou
Llucalari
3,5
Son Bou
Basílica
Paleocristiana
Sant Llorenç
Cap de ses Penyes
Cala de Llucalari
Torre Llissà
So na Caçana
6
Cala de St. Llorenç
5
★
4
4,5
Me1
Biniadrix
E
130
128
Cales
Coves
Son Vitamina
del Mar
Cala En
Porter
Cala en Porter

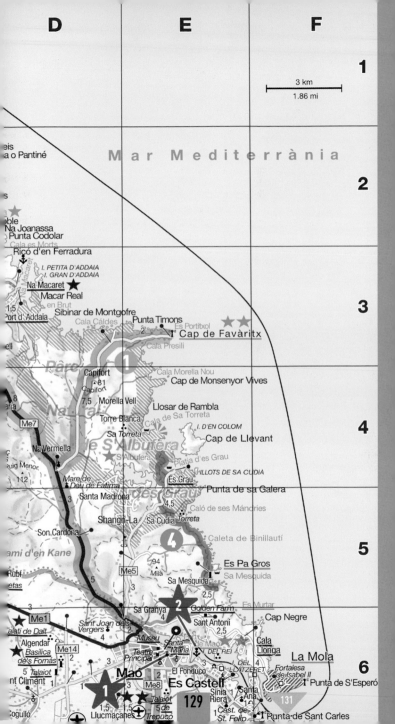

D E F

1

3 km
1.86 mi

eis
a o Pantiné

M a r   M e d i t e r r à n i a

2

s

ble
Na Joanassa
Punta Codolar
Cala es Morts
Ricó d'en Ferradura
I. PETITA D'ADDAIA
I. GRAN D'ADDAIA
Na Macaret
Macar Real
1,5   en Brut
Port d'Addaia   Sibinar de Montgofre

3

Cala Cáldes   Punta Timons   Es Portitxol   ★★
ell   2   Cap de Favàritx
Cala Presili
Pàrc   Cala Morella Nou
Capifort   Cap de Monsenyor Vives
·81
Capifort
7,5   Morella Vell
·8   Llosar de Rambla
aria   Torre Blanca   Cala de Sa Torreta
Me7   Sa Torreta   *I. D'EN COLOM*
de S'Albufera   Cap de Llevant
Na Vermella   S'Albufera
Puig Menor   Platja d'es Grau
·112   Mare de   *ILLOTS DE SA CUDIA*
Déu de Fatima   Es Grau
Santa Madrona   Punta de sa Galera
3   descgrau
Shangri-La   Sa Cudia   Torreta
Son Cardona   Caló de ses Mándries
Caleta de Binillautí
ami d'en Kane
94
Rubí   Milà   Me5
etas   Es Pa Gros
3   Sa Mesquida   Sa Mesquida
5   3
2,5
3   Sa Granya   Es Murtar
★   Me1   Golden Farm   Cap Negre
Sant Joan des   4   Sant Antoni
alati de Dalt   Vergers   2,5
4   2   Cala
Algendar   Museu   Llonga
Basilica   Teatre   Santa   La Mola
de's Fornàs   Me14   Principal   Maria   DEL REI
3   El Fonduco   *I. DEL*   Fortalesa
5   Talaiot   2   *LLATZERET*   de Isabel II   Punta de S'Esperó
nt Climent   1   Me8   Es Castell
Mao   Sinia   Santa
Cogulló   3   Riera   Ana   131
1,5   Talaiot   Cast. de
Llucmaçanes   5 de   St. Felip   Punta de Sant Carles
Trepucó

129

4

5

6

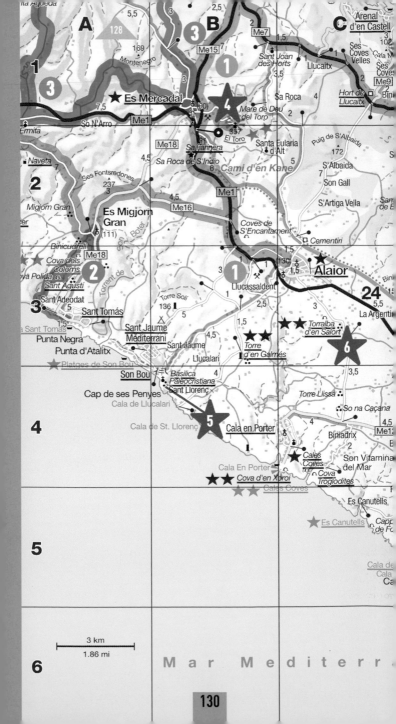

KEY TO ROAD ATLAS

Autobahn · Gebührenpflichtige Anschlussstelle · Gebührenstelle · Anschlussstelle mit Nummer · Rasthaus mit Übernachtung · Raststätte · Kleinraststätte · Tankstelle · Parkplatz mit und ohne WC	Trento	Motorway · Toll junction · Toll station · Junction with number · Motel · Restaurant · Snackbar · Filling-station · Parking place with and without WC
Autobahn in Bau und geplant mit Datum der voraussichtlichen Verkehrsübergabe	Datum Date	Motorway under construction and projected with expected date of opening
Zweibahnige Straße (4-spurig)		Dual carriageway (4 lanes)
Fernverkehrsstraße · Straßennummern	14 E45	Trunk road · Road numbers
Wichtige Hauptstraße		Important main road
Hauptstraße · Tunnel · Brücke	)=(	Main road · Tunnel · Bridge
Nebenstraßen		Minor roads
Fahrweg · Fußweg		Track · Footpath
Wanderweg (Auswahl)	----------	Tourist footpath (selection)
Eisenbahn mit Fernverkehr		Main line railway
Zahnradbahn, Standseilbahn		Rack-railway, funicular
Kabinenschwebebahn · Sessellift		Aerial cableway · Chair-lift
Autofähre · Personenfähre		Car ferry · Passenger ferry
Schifffahrtslinie		Shipping route
Naturschutzgebiet · Sperrgebiet		Nature reserve · Prohibited area
Nationalpark · Naturpark · Wald		National park · natural park · Forest
Straße für Kfz. gesperrt	X X X X X X	Road closed to motor vehicles
Straße mit Gebühr		Toll road
Straße mit Wintersperre	XII-II	Road closed in winter
Straße für Wohnanhänger gesperrt bzw. nicht empfehlenswert		Road closed or not recommended for caravans
Touristenstraße · Pass	Weinstraße ⌃1510	Tourist route · Pass
Schöner Ausblick · Rundblick · Landschaftlich bes. schöne Strecke		Scenic view · Panoramic view · Route with beautiful scenery
Heilbad · Schwimmbad	♨	Spa · Swimming pool
Jugendherberge · Campingplatz	△ ⋏ ⋏	Youth hostel · Camping site
Golfplatz · Sprungschanze		Golf-course · Ski jump
Kirche im Ort, freistehend · Kapelle	♦	Church · Chapel
Kloster · Klosterruine		Monastery · Monastery ruin
Synagoge · Moschee	✡	Synagogue · Mosque
Schloss, Burg · Schloss-, Burgruine		Palace, castle · Ruin
Turm · Funk-, Fernsehturm		Tower · Radio-, TV-tower
Leuchtturm · Kraftwerk		Lighthouse · Power station
Wasserfall · Schleuse		Waterfall · Lock
Bauwerk · Marktplatz, Areal	▪ ▫	Important building · Market place, area
Ausgrabungs- u. Ruinenstätte · Bergwerk	⚒	Arch. excavation, ruins · Mine
Dolmen · Menhir · Nuraghen	π Ω	Dolmen · Menhir · Nuraghe
Hünen-, Hügelgrab · Soldatenfriedhof	☆	Cairn · Military cemetery
Hotel, Gasthaus, Berghütte · Höhle	⌂ ∩	Hotel, inn, refuge · Cave

Kultur / Culture

Kultur Malerisches Ortsbild · Ortshöhe	WIEN (171)	**Culture** Picturesque town · Elevation
Eine Reise wert	★★ MILANO	Worth a journey
Lohnt einen Umweg	★ TEMPLIN	Worth a detour
Sehenswert	Andermatt	Worth seeing

Landschaft / Landscape

Landschaft Eine Reise wert	★★ Las Cañadas	**Landscape** Worth a journey
Lohnt einen Umweg	★ Texel	Worth a detour
Sehenswert	Dikti	Worth seeing

MARCO POLO Erlebnistour 1		**MARCO POLO Discovery Tour 1**
MARCO POLO Erlebnistouren		**MARCO POLO Discovery Tours**
MARCO POLO Highlight	★	**MARCO POLO Highlight**

FOR YOUR NEXT TRIP...

MARCO POLO TRAVEL GUIDES

The travel guides with
Insider Tips

INDEX

This index lists all towns, bays, destinations and estates as well as names and keywords featured in this guide. Numbers in bold indicate a main entry.

CREDITS

WRITE TO US

e-mail: info@marcopologuides.co.uk

Did you have a great holiday?
Is there something on your mind?
Whatever it is, let us know!
Whether you want to praise, alert us
to errors or give us a personal tip –
MARCO POLO would be pleased to
hear from you.
We do everything we can to provide the
very latest information for your trip.

Nevertheless, despite all of our authors'
thorough research, errors can creep in.
MARCO POLO does not accept any
liability for this. Please contact us by
e-mail or post.

MARCO POLO Travel Publishing Ltd
Pinewood, Chineham Business Park
Crockford Lane, Chineham
Basingstoke, Hampshire RG24 8AL
United Kingdom

PICTURE CREDITS
Cover photograph: Cala Galdana beach (mauritius images: World Pictures)
Photos: DMS Sports & Kayak: David Mascaró Soriano (19 top); DuMont Bildarchiv: Schröder (113); Ecològic de Menorca: Xavier Diari Menorca (18 top); f1online/AGE: (29), G. Azumendi (11), R. Campillo (30); Getty Images: Imgorthand (106/107), G. Schuster (18 bottom); huber-images: G. Croppi (17), R. Schmid (5, 14/15, 20/21, 34, 52/53, 59, 61, 62/63, 69, 74/75, 80/81, 82); F. Ihlow (112 bottom, 124/125); © iStockphoto: Eric Foltz (18 centre); Laif: M. Amme (89, 102/103), Huber (54, 110, 112 top), G. Knechtel (40); Laif/Le Figaro Magazine: Martin (2/3, 98); Look: H. Leue (7, 37), K. Maeritz (flap left, 70/71, 90/91), Richter (flap right); Look/age fotostock (8, 9, 22, 32/33, 56, 64, 76); K. Maeritz (43, 78); mauritius images: S. Beuthan (25, 67, 110/111), Siepmann (104/105), J. Warburton-Lee (51); mauritius images/age (4 bottom, 6, 26/27, 44, 95); mauritius images/Alamy (28 left, 30/31, 31, 38, 47, 73, 109); mauritius images/Axiom Photographic (85); mauritius images/CuboImages (28 right); mauritius images/Robert Harding (48); mauritius images/Westend61 (4 top, 19 bottom, 86); mauritius images: World Pictures (1); K. Thiele (111); vario images/Axiom (12/13); White Star: M. Gumm (10)

2nd Edition – fully revised and updated 2017
Worldwide Distribution: Marco Polo Travel Publishing Ltd, Pinewood, Chineham Business Park, Crockford Lane, Basingstoke, Hampshire RG24 8AL, United Kingdom. E-mail: sales@marcopolouk.com
© MAIRDUMONT GmbH & Co. KG, Ostfildern
Chief editor: Marion Zorn
Author: Jörg Dörpinghaus, co-author: Izabella Gawin; editor: Jochen Schürmann
Programme supervision: Susanne Heimburger, Tamara Hub, Nikolai Michaelis, Kristin Schimpf, Martin Silbermann
Picture editor: Gabriele Forst, Anja Schlatterer; What's hot: wunder media, Munich
Cartography road atlas & pull-out map: © MAIRDUMONT, Ostfildern
Design: milchhof: atelier, Berlin; Front cover, pull-out map cover, page 1: factor product Munich; Discovery Tours: Susan Chaaban, Dipl.Des (FH)
Translated from German by Neil Williamson; Susan Jones; editor of the English edition: Margaret Howie, fullproof.co.za
Prepress: writehouse, Cologne; InterMedia, Ratingen
Phrase book in cooperation with Ernst Klett Sprachen GmbH, Stuttgart, Editorial by Pons Wörterbücher

DOS & DON'TS ✋

Here are a few things to look out for on your Menorca holiday

DO TAKE CARE WHEN SWIMMING

The sea south of Menorca is particularly well-known for strong currents which can be treacherous, especially off the larger, open beaches. Always observe the warning buoys and do not swim out too far. The north of the island can be dangerous when the *tramuntana* is blowing. Observe the red warning flag on the beaches! In recent years in summer there have been repeated occurrences of jellyfish which can cause painful stinging. Here too you should observe the warnings on supervised beaches.

DON'T BUY FROM HAWKERS

They suddenly appear on the beach: hawkers offering a wide range of fruits or drinks. They hardly ever satisfy the official health and safety requirements. Better not to buy anything!

DON'T CLIMB OVER WALLS

Not every Menorcan is happy to see strangers walking across his property. Occasionally a shot gun has even been drawn, more often the dogs are let loose. This is why you absolutely must speak to the owner before setting off on a hike or looking for somewhere to camp "rough". On marked hiking trails, always make sure you close the gate behind you as you cross private property.

DON'T RUSH

"Ets Menorca, no frissis!" ("slow down, you are on Menorca") is what the locals like to tell you. Or: "Poc a poc" – "Take it easy!" More patience, less speed is the motto on this island which applies when driving or even when ordering food in the restaurant...

DO BE WARY OF FLOWER GIRLS

In addition to the well-known shell game players, "flower girls" also operate in the tourist resorts in summer. They try to offer flowers to holidaymakers who in turn – disarmed by such kindness – quite often take out their purse or wallet. This opportunity is used by the flower girls to help themselves in the confusion or in the tourists' eagerness to communicate. It is far better to avoid the "friendly" girls in the first place or, if they are being particularly insistent, shout loudly for the police (*policia!*).

DO SAVE WATER

The water table on Menorca has sunk alarmingly in recent years and many wells are already contaminated by salt. As a tourist you too can help save water by using tap water sparingly.